HELLO, CUPCAKE!

HELLO,

HOUGHTON MIFFLIN COMPANY
Boston New York

CUPCAKE!

Karen Tack and Alan Richardson

TEXT AND PHOTOGRAPHS BY ALAN RICHARDSON
RECIPES AND FOOD STYLING BY KAREN TACK

For Chris, Erik, and Liam,
the sprinkles on my cupcakes
—K.T.

For Larry
and his tremendous devotion to dessert
—A.R.

All trademarks in this book are the property of their respective owners.

Visit our website: www.houghtonmifflinbooks.com.

For information about permission to reproduce selections from this book, write to Permissions, Houghton Mifflin Company, 215 Park Avenue South, New York, New York 10003.

Book design by Anne Chalmers

Typeface: Helvetica Neue

Copyright © 2008 by Karen Tack and Alan Richardson

Printed in China • C&C 10 9 8 7 6 5 4 3 2

Library of Congress Cataloging-in-Publication Data

Richardson, Alan, date.
  Hello, cupcake! / Karen Tack and Alan Richardson ;
  text and photographs by Alan Richardson ;
  recipes and food styling by Karen Tack.
    p. cm.
  ISBN-13: 978-0-618-82925-5 (alk. paper)
  ISBN-10: 0-618-82925-3 (alk. paper)
    1. Cupcakes. 2. Cake decorating. I. Tack, Karen.
  II. Title.
  TX771.R52 2008
  641.8'653—dc22   2007040029

ACKNOWLEDGMENTS

We didn't get this cupcake crazy on our own. We want to thank the many editors and art directors who collaborated with us over the years and contributed their own zany ideas. Whether working with you as a team or separately, we've picked up a lot of inspiration from all of you. A special thanks to Doug Turshen for first stimulating our cupcake imagination and also to Susan Westmoreland, Babs Chernetz, Frank Melodia, Marisol Vera, Ruth Reichl, Richard Ferretti, Erika Oliveira, Romulo Yanes, Sally Lee, Clare Lissaman, Linda Fears, Shelley Wolson, Kate Keating, Diane Lamphron, Jackie Plant, Fraya Berg, Karmen Lizzul, Betsy Jordan, Stephanie Saible, Wendy Smolen, Rena Coyle, Tom Eckerle, Cheryl Slocum, Jan Hazard, Jane Chestnut, and Brad Pallas for making sure our cupcakes never lost their creative edge.

We've called on many friends to look at projects and give us a thumbs-up (or down). Special thanks to Allison and Rebecca Kural, Sarah Morris (future cupcaker extraordinaire), Jennifer Hess and Louise Rooney (our biggest fans), Richard and Sherry Zucker (our in-house marketing team), Carol Schwartz (our groupie), and Chris Raymond and Lynne Palazzi (our hometown publishing touchstones). Friends, school chums, and families in Riverside, Connecticut: thanks for taking care of all those extra cupcakes we had lying around.

Our friend Carol Prager has been cheering, advising, counseling, and nurturing this project for a great many years, and we're sure she's glad it's finally finished.

Without Ellie Ritt and Roy Galaday backing us with their amazing creativity, we'd be lost. Thanks to both of you for all your help.

Karen's mother-in-law, Barbara Tack, is a talented artist, and we're proud of the beautiful painting she made of our family tree (see page 154). We hope she approves of our rendition of her (on the tree's lower-left-hand limb). As for the rest of our families, thanks for putting up with all the candy and cupcakes around the house. We want you to know how much we appreciate all of the support and love. Karen's older son, Erik, constantly graded our efforts. Thanks for giving us more A's than C's. Karen's husband, Chris, is a man of extreme patience and turned our mania into his passion. Even when the Tack home overflowed with old cupcakes, Chris took it all in stride and offered advice, encouragement, and a beer. Karen's younger son, Liam, doesn't really like cupcakes, but he was always available when we needed to dispose of an extra gummy bear. Alan's partner, Larry Frascella, was the best family editor we could want. He offered insight and astute comments on the writing and photos and kept us on our toes every step of the way. Laura Mecca and the kids, Sarah, Anna, Lawrence, Stephanie, and Thomas, tested and tasted their way through a good many of our projects and proved that Long Island kids make great cupcakers. Karen's parents, Joan and Bill McCoy, and siblings Kirk and Kim shaped her candy-colored vision and taught her to never say no to a cupcake. Alan's family in Mississippi has been a constant reminder that things (including cupcakes) are always sweeter down South.

Rux Martin has been a great friend and editor, and we love her for it. Her entire team at Houghton Mifflin has been terrific, and we want to thank Michaela Sullivan for our striking cover and Anne Chalmers for the beautiful design of our book.

Martha Kaplan must be the best agent on earth; she loved every project we showed to her. Thanks, Martha.

A big shout-out to the cookie and candy companies that have been busy creating all of the wonderful goodies that make cupcaking so much fun. Keep it coming.

And last but not least, to our cupcake mascots—Bunny, Karen's wheaten terrier, and Lucky, Alan's silver schnauzer. Through it all, you guys kept the floors clean.

CONTENTS

Meet the
Buttinskys

INTRODUCTION

WITH JUST A HANDFUL OF CANDIES, a can of frosting, a ziplock bag, and some cupcake batter, you are on your way to having fun with those pesky Buttinskys next door, planting a garden of spring vegetables so sweet even the kids will eat them, or turning your next pool party into a shark attack. When the mailman tires of your snarling dog, meet him at the end of the drive with a terrier cupcake before he goes postal. If your son brings home a D in biology, send him to school with a platter of insect cupcakes to show he's ready to get down to business. Want to see the inside of your new neighbor's house? Send her a bouquet of sunflower cupcakes to break the ice.

Make our cupcakes for a holiday or a special event, and they'll provide the entertainment. Play an April Fool's trick on the family with a cupcake TV dinner. At the neighborhood Halloween party, hand out alien cupcakes oozing with neon frosting and sitting in their own spaceships. When you want a little more sophistication, our black and white cupcakes are refined enough to serve with champagne.

All this is easy: honest. Forget the complicated pastry techniques and expensive decorating supplies. You can find almost everything for these projects at your local grocery store, drugstore, or even a gas-station convenience store (which often has some of the most extensive selections of candies). M&M's work equally well as noses, eyes, or ears. A circus peanut candy transforms into a horse's head, or a clown's floppy shoe. For finishing your designs, a ziplock bag makes a great disposable piping bag.

You don't need any baking skills to make these projects either. We've come up with a simple formula for doctoring a cake mix. No one will suspect you didn't make these cupcakes from scratch, and they have a uniformly firm surface that won't pull apart when you frost them. And as for the frosting, we have yet to find a homemade one that has the versatility of canned. Store-bought frostings take well to tinting, making it simple to create vibrant colors. They were born for microwaving, melting into a consistently smooth texture for dipping.

We've also provided recipes for the simplest, most delicious homemade cupcakes possible, as well as for some of the best-tasting frostings you'll ever find.

So find a project that tickles your fancy, grab a bag or two of candy, and get ready to put your smile into overdrive. It's time to get this party started.

IT'S JUST AN

Mix and match the hair, eyes, and mouth

wild

mild

stringy

straight

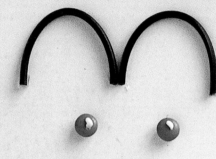

wide

beady

open

silly

heart

circle

slice

wavy

EXPRESSION!

and choose an expression to make a favorite face.

multi   **straw**   **mocha**   **flame**

angry   **goofy**   **bashful**   **moody**

sad   **quiet**   **happy**   **nice**

ESSENTIAL TOOLS

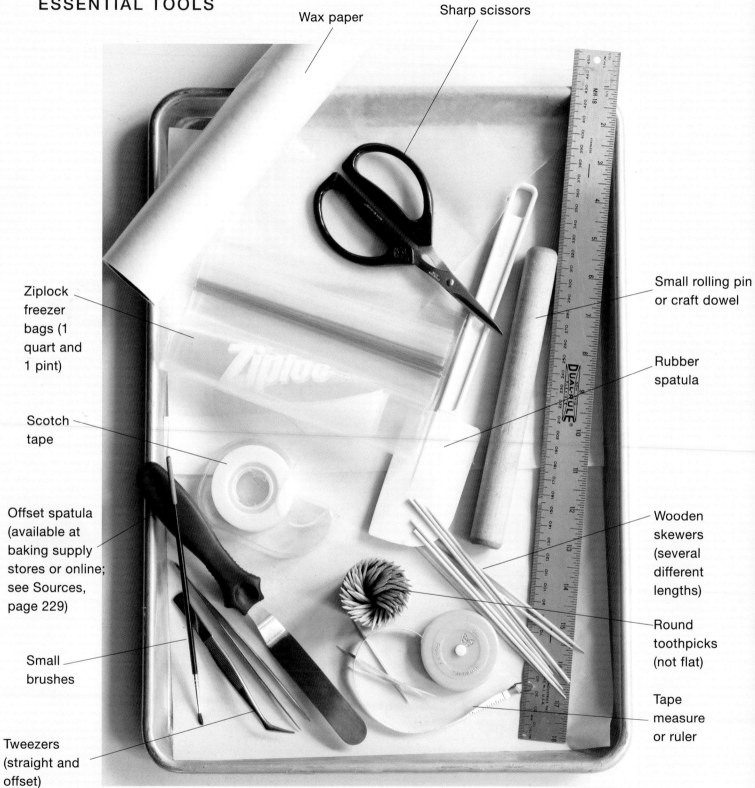

Wax paper

Sharp scissors

Ziplock freezer bags (1 quart and 1 pint)

Small rolling pin or craft dowel

Rubber spatula

Scotch tape

Offset spatula (available at baking supply stores or online; see Sources, page 229)

Wooden skewers (several different lengths)

Small brushes

Round toothpicks (not flat)

Tweezers (straight and offset)

Tape measure or ruler

YOUR
DESIGN MATERIALS

SPRINKLEABLES

A galaxy of decorations made from sugar or candy can be used for edging a cupcake, coating the surface, or sprinkling on top.

DESIGNABLES
Just pick your
favorite color
and press these
treats into the
frosting.

CUTTABLES

These colorful candies are easily cut with scissors, a small knife, or a cookie cutter.

New!
Twizzlers
Rainbow Twists

NET WT 1.9 OZ (53 g)

ROLLABLES

Semisoft and pliable, these candies can be molded, rolled, and cut into odd shapes and design elements.

CUPCAKING TECHNIQUES

FILLING CUPCAKE CUPS

Our favorite tool, the ziplock bag, is great for filling cupcake liners. It makes it simple to measure out the batter and to place it exactly in the center of the liners without spilling or dribbling. Freezer-weight bags work best because they are extra-thick. Use two 1-quart ziplock freezer bags. A standard recipe mix will fill 2 bags.

Fold the edges back 1 inch and place each bag in a container, such as a 1-quart plastic deli container, to hold it upright and open.

Divide the batter evenly between the bags. Unfold the edges of each bag, press out the excess air, and seal.

Grasp the bag below the zipped edge, pushing the batter down toward one corner. Snip off about 1/2 inch of the corner.

Put the cut opening in the center of a cupcake liner, squeeze gently, and fill the cup two-thirds full. As the batter approaches that level, stop applying pressure and remove the tip from the cup.

Use a rubber spatula or other flat tool to squeegee the last of the batter down to the cut corner, and continue piping.

SPREADING FROSTING

Creating a perfectly smooth or nicely swirled top is a cinch. Your aim is to spread the frosting up to but not over the edge of the paper liner and to glue down the crumbs in the process. Then you can make the surface as flat or fancy as you like. With frosting, less is never more.

Make sure your frosting is at room temperature; it will have a better texture and be easier to handle. And always stir the frosting before using it.

Place a generous dollop of frosting in the center of the cupcake.

Push it away from you to the edge with a spatula, working your way around the cupcake.

Holding the center portion of the blade at a slight angle, remove any excess frosting and smooth the top.

At the end of a smooth stroke, keep the blade flat and pull to the side to avoid lifting the frosting into peaks. If the top needs more smoothing, wipe the spatula clean and swipe again.

For a swirled peak, hold the tip of the blade at a higher angle. Make a swirl stroke, pulling the tip straight up.

To center the peak, work the spatula tip in a spiral from the outer edge to the center, then lift.

For a mounded top, use an extra-large dollop of frosting.

Hold the cupcake by its paper base in one hand and grasp the spatula in the other. Spread the frosting with a clockwise motion, while turning the cupcake counterclockwise. Work in long continuous strokes.

MAKING DESIGNS WITH FROSTING

A ziplock bag is much more efficient and easy to use than a real piping bag. The frosting is zipped in place, so it won't leak all over your hand. Changing the tip is no big deal; all you do is snip a new corner. By making different-shaped cuts in the corner of the bag, you can create grass, hair, fur, or monograms.

EDGING CUPCAKES

Edging the frosted cupcake in sugar, cookie crumbs, sprinkles, or chopped nuts hides any imperfections and adds color and texture to the cupcake.

Place a large amount of sugar or other ingredient in a small shallow bowl.

While the frosting is still moist, hold the cupcake by its base and carefully roll the edge in the sugar. Press the frosting against the sugar to smooth out any imperfections.

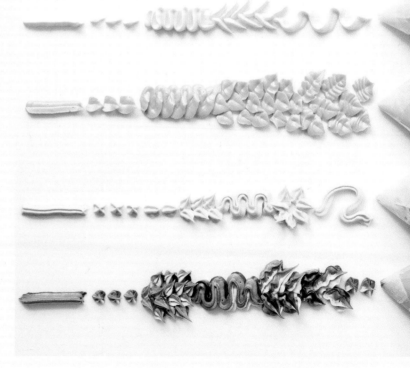

FILLING A ZIPLOCK BAG

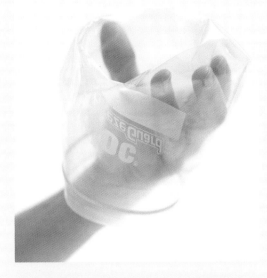

To fill the ziplock, hold the bottom of the bag in one hand and fold about half of the bag inside out over your hand.

Using a spatula, fill the area of the bag inside your hand. Lift the edges of the bag up and around the frosting, press out the excess air, and seal the bag.

Grasp the bag by the zippered edge and squeeze the frosting down to one corner.

For fancy designs, reinforce the corner with 6 overlapping layers of Scotch tape.

Pinch the taped corner flat. For a plain tip, use scissors to snip a very small ($1/16$-inch) corner off the bottom.

cupcaking techniques ● 13

CUTTING A TIP

Fill the ziplock bag with frosting, press out the excess air, and seal. (Use 2 bags and 2 colors if you're doing both leaves and petals.)

Push the frosting down to one corner. Reinforce the corner of the bag with 6 overlapping layers of Scotch tape. Pinch the taped corner flat. Use scissors to snip off a small V-shape, M-shape, or plain cut from the corner.

MAKING LEAVES AND PETALS

Starting on the perimeter of the cupcake, place the tip flat on the surface of the cupcake. Squeeze the bag, pulling away from the center of the cupcake. Use small side-to-side pushes or wiggles to make the leaf or petal shape. Work toward the center in concentric circles, overlapping the pattern slightly.

Starting on the perimeter of the cupcake, place the tip of the bag on the surface, squeeze, release the pressure, and pull the frosting away from the cupcake. Continue piping in concentric circles, slightly overlapping the pattern as you move toward the center.

MAKING FUR

For multicolor fur, you'll need 2 to 3 colors of frosting.

Hold the ziplock bag open in your hand and spread a thick line of each of 2 colors of frosting up opposite sides of the bag. Fill the bag down the center with the third color if using. Press out the excess air and seal the bag, making sure all 3 colors are pushed down to one corner.

Reinforce the corner of the bag with 6 layers of Scotch tape. Pinch the taped corner flat. Use scissors to snip a small (1/8-inch) M-shape in the corner by cutting 2 small V's side by side (see opposite page).

MAKING MULTIPLE-COLOR FROSTING

Fill each ziplock bag with tinted frosting, using as many bags and colors as desired. Snip a 1/8-inch corner from each bag.

Start piping the design in one color. Add the second color on top of or next to the first color. Use the tip of the bag to blend the two together. Continue with the remaining colors, overlapping and mixing them as you go.

DRAWING AND GLUING

Melting wafers harden like chocolate and look like chocolate but are much easier to work with. You can use them to draw things as varied as hair, wings, bones, safety pins, monograms, and spiderwebs. They're available in a wide variety of colors from specialty stores, some grocery stores, and online (see Sources, page 229). Chips made from white chocolate, peanut butter, and butterscotch can also be used to draw and glue. Real chocolate works too, but it may streak and discolor when heated, is harder to handle at room temperature, and must be kept refrigerated until ready to be served.

Place the candy melting wafers or other candies in a ziplock bag. Do not seal.

Place the bag in the microwave for 10 seconds. Remove and massage to blend and work out any lumps. (Always handle carefully in case the candy has overheated.) If the candy isn't completely softened, microwave for 10 seconds more, and check again. Repeat as necessary.

Press out the excess air in the bag and seal. Push the mixture down to one corner. Snip a $1/16$-inch corner from the bag.

The melted wafers can also be used as glue—when assembling bug bodies and legs, for example. Place the decorative candies in the melted wafer glue before it hardens.

Make a template by drawing a cupcake-sized circle with a pencil; a standard cupcake is about 3 inches across and a mini is 2 inches. Draw the outline of your design in marker. Place the template on a cookie sheet and cover with wax paper.

Using the ziplock bag, trace the design on the template to create an outline of the drawing on the wax paper.

Fill in the outline with the melted candy. Swirl or layer the melted candy to give it shape and texture. Tap the sheet pan gently to flatten the surface.

Allow the drawing to harden in the refrigerator for several minutes. Carefully remove it from the wax paper and place it on the frosted cupcake.

Has anyone seen Elvis?

Colonel Sanders or Santa?

Goldilocks

BUILDING WITH CUPCAKES

Choose snacks that have interesting shapes, like mini doughnuts, doughnut holes, Mallomars, Twinkies, and creme wafers. Frosting is the mortar that holds the shapes together. Once the whole structure is finished, place it in the freezer to chill until the frosting is firm. This step is crucial to prevent the constructions from coming apart when they are dipped in slightly warm frosting.

DIPPING CUPCAKES

For a firm, shiny surface or a glistening, smooth one, we recommend canned frosting, which holds up well to the heat and maintains a perfect texture when melted. Avoid whipped frostings or those with bits of coconut or nuts. You can tint the frosting if you want.

Place the frosting in a 1- to 2-cup microwavable measuring cup. Microwave for 5 to 10 seconds—no more.

Test by dipping a spoon into the frosting and letting it run back into the cup. It should be the consistency of lightly whipped cream or Elmer's glue. If it's too thick, stir and microwave for 5 to 10 seconds more. (Handle with care.)

Repeat if necessary, microwaving for 5 to 10 seconds at a time and stirring. Be careful not to overheat the frosting, however, or it will separate.

When the frosting thickens, return it to the microwave and zap for 5 to 10 seconds.

You can also check the consistency by running your finger through the frosting on the back of the spoon. It should coat the spoon smoothly but be thick enough to hold the edges of the pattern of your finger.

Hold the cupcake by its bottom and dip the top in the melted frosting up to the edge of the paper liner.

Lift the cupcake and allow the excess frosting to drip off.

Quickly turn the cupcake upright.

You can pop any small bubbles with a toothpick, but little imperfections are natural and make your cupcakes look deliciously homemade.

CUTTING COOKIES
FOR CUPCAKE DESIGNS

Use a small paring knife to whittle, shape, and make detailed cuts. Use a small-toothed serrated steak knife to make broad cuts and to cut sandwich cookies. Use a gentle sawing motion, taking care not to crack or crush the cookie.

Microwaving the cookie for a few seconds will soften it, making intricate cuts easier.

MULTIPLE CUPCAKE DESIGNS

For larger designs, we like to make our assemblies match a multiple of 24, since that is how many cupcakes a store-bought cake mix produces.

Draw the circles of the cupcakes as they will appear in the whole design and label them with their decorations.

Following the template, place the unfrosted cupcakes in position.

Lay the decorations on top of the unfrosted cupcakes to make sure the design works.

Remove, frost, and decorate the cupcakes one at a time before placing them back in the design.

When the final cupcake is in place, add any decorations that cross over from one cupcake to another.

→ CHOC. WAFER

→ MINI M&M'S

→ NECCO WAFER

→ FROSTING ON COOKIE

→ GUM BALL

SUGARED →

→ PIROUETTES

SUGARED

→ GUM BALL

→ CHOC. COOKIE

→ CHOC. COOKIE

→ CHOC. ALMONDS

April Fool's

If we had to pick only one holiday to last all year, we would choose April Fool's. Serve up these fool-the-eye cupcakes and watch for the double take. Sometimes what you see is not what you get!

CORN ON THE COB

Our corniest project ever! The ears are bursting with fresh summer flavor. But surprise: those kernels are jelly beans, the butter pats are fruit chews, and the salt and pepper is black and white sugar.

24 vanilla cupcakes baked in white paper liners

1 can (16 ounces) vanilla frosting
  Yellow food coloring
  About 3¹/₂ cups small jelly beans (Jelly Bellys) in
    assorted yellow, cream, and white colors
4 pieces yellow fruit chews (Laffy Taffys, Starbursts)
1 tablespoon each black and white decorating sugars
  (available at baking supply stores or see Sources,
  page 229)
8 sets of corn holders (optional)

1. Tint the vanilla frosting pale yellow with the food coloring.

2. Working with 3 cupcakes at a time, spread yellow frosting on top of each. Arrange about 5 rows of jelly beans, close together, on each cupcake. Place the 3 cupcakes side by side on a corn dish or a serving platter. Repeat with the remaining cupcakes, frosting, and jelly beans.

3. Cut the fruit chews into eight 1-inch squares, and soften the edges slightly by hand so that they look melted. Place 1 square on top of each group of 3 cupcakes. Sprinkle with the sugars. Insert 1 corn holder, if using, in each of the end cupcakes.

BAGELS AND LOX

Where's the Sunday paper? This bagel is a mini doughnut with a schmear of vanilla frosting. Add a slice of orange fruit-chew lox, sprinkle with scallions of green licorice, and serve with a wedge of candy lemon on the side.

24 Lemon Poppy-Seed Cupcakes (page 224) baked in
    pale yellow paper liners

24 plain mini doughnuts
 2 tablespoons light corn syrup
 1 tablespoon poppy seeds
24 orange fruit chews (Starbursts)
 1 can (16 ounces) vanilla frosting
   Yellow food coloring
 4 strands green licorice twists (Twizzlers Rainbow
    Twists), thinly sliced diagonally
24 mini candy lemon slices

1. Cut the doughnuts in half horizontally to make the bagels. Heat the corn syrup in a small bowl in the microwave until bubbly, 5 to 10 seconds. Brush the top of the doughnuts with the corn syrup. Sprinkle lightly with the poppy seeds and set aside.

2. Soften several orange fruit chews at a time in the microwave for 2 to 3 seconds. Roll out each fruit chew on a sheet of wax paper to a 2½-by-1¼-inch rectangle. Score the top lengthwise with a knife.

3. Spread a thin layer of the vanilla frosting on the cut side of the bottom half of each doughnut. Arrange 1 fruit chew, folded slightly to look like lox, on top.

4. Tint the remaining vanilla frosting yellow with the food coloring and spread on top of the cupcakes. Place the bottom half of 1 doughnut on each cupcake. Scatter a few licorice slices over the doughnut and place 1 doughnut half with poppy seeds on top. Serve with a candy lemon slice on the side.

BUTTERED POPCORN

Rent a movie and pass the popcorn! This prank uses white and yellow mini marshmallows to create buttered popcorn clusters.

36 mini vanilla cupcakes baked in white paper liners

1 can (16 ounces) vanilla frosting

3 cups white mini marshmallows (from a 10.5-ounce bag)

1 cup yellow mini marshmallows (from a 10.5-ounce multicolored bag)

3 popcorn boxes half filled with crumpled tissue paper (available at party stores; or see Sources, page 229; optional)

1. Line two cookie sheets with wax paper. Spoon $1/4$ cup of the vanilla frosting into a ziplock bag. Press out the excess air and close the bag.

2. For each piece of popcorn, use 2 marshmallows of the same color. Using clean scissors, cut 1 marshmallow into thirds, crosswise. Arrange the pieces on the cookie sheet in the shape of a three-leaf clover, pressing gently with your fingertips to flatten slightly. Snip a $1/8$-inch corner from the bag and pipe a dot of frosting on one end of the second marshmallow. Press the other marshmallow into the center of the cloverleaf arrangement; the frosting will hold the 4 pieces together. Repeat with the remaining white and yellow marshmallows until you have 225 to 250 pieces of popcorn.

3. Spread the tops of the mini cupcakes with the remaining vanilla frosting. Press 6 or 7 popcorn pieces onto the top of each cupcake. Any loose pieces can be secured with a dot of frosting from the ziplock bag.

4. Let the cupcakes sit for about 30 minutes before stacking them in the popcorn boxes or a bowl.

TV DINNER

Makes 3 drumsticks,
1 mashed potatoes, 1 peas and carrots,
and 1 chocolate pudding: 6 cupcakes

No need to worry about your peas and carrots mixing with your chocolate pudding in this TV dinner . . . it's all made with candy and sugar. Go ahead and grab a chicken leg by its white chocolate bone, or dig into the pile of frosting mashed potatoes topped with caramel gravy. You might want to save the vegetables for last, because the peas and carrots are actually Runts and Starbursts.

6 vanilla cupcakes baked in silver foil liners

Disposable aluminum cupcake baking tray (available
   at grocery stores)

DRUMSTICKS

1/4 cup white chocolate melting wafers (available at
   baking supply stores or see Sources, page 229)
1 cup vanilla frosting
3 plain doughnut holes
1 cup cornflake crumbs

1. Place the bone template (page 33) on a cookie sheet. Cover with wax paper. Place the white chocolate melting wafers in a ziplock bag. Do not seal the bag. Microwave for about 10 seconds to soften. Massage the mixture and return to the microwave. Repeat the process until the chocolate is smooth. Press out the excess air and seal the bag. Snip a 1/8-inch corner from the bag and, following the bone template, pipe an outline on the wax paper. Fill in the bone with chocolate (see page 16). Tap the pan lightly to smooth the top of the chocolate. Repeat with the remaining chocolate to make 3 bones. (You may want to make extra bones in case one breaks.) Refrigerate until firm, about 5 minutes.

2. Spread vanilla frosting on top of 3 cupcakes, mounding it slightly (see page 11). Place 1 doughnut hole on top of each cupcake. Spread frosting over the doughnut hole until it is smooth and covered (see page 18).

3. Place the cornflake crumbs in a medium bowl and gently press the frosted cupcakes into the crumbs to cover completely. Place the cupcakes in the aluminum baking tray.

4. Using a sharp knife, make a small slit in the top of each crumbed doughnut hole. Carefully peel 1 chocolate bone from the wax paper and insert the pointed end into one of the slits. Repeat with the remaining 2 bones and cupcakes.

MASHED POTATOES

   1 **yellow fruit chew (Laffy Taffys, Starbursts)**
   3 **tablespoons vanilla frosting**
1$^1/_2$ **tablespoons caramel sauce**

1. Cut the yellow fruit chew into a 1-inch square.

2. Spread the vanilla frosting on 1 cupcake, mounding it slightly (see page 11). Use a small spoon to create a well in the center of the frosting. Place the cupcake in the baking tray.

3. Place the fruit chew in the well at an angle. Heat the caramel sauce for 2 to 4 seconds in the microwave and drizzle it on top of the cupcake so that it fills the well and spills over like gravy.

PEAS AND CARROTS

   3 **orange fruit chews (Tootsie Fruit Rolls, Starbursts)**
   2 **tablespoons vanilla frosting**
   Green food coloring
   2 **tablespoons hard green candies (Runts)**

1. Cut the fruit chews into $^1/_4$-inch cubes.

2. Tint the vanilla frosting bright green with the food coloring and spread on top of 1 cupcake. Arrange the green candies and orange chews on top of the cupcake, pressing them into the frosting. Place the cupcake in the baking tray.

CHOCOLATE PUDDING

3 tablespoons chocolate frosting

1 teaspoon colored jimmies

1. Spoon the chocolate frosting into a ziplock bag, press out the excess air, and seal. Snip a ¼-inch corner from the bag. Pipe the chocolate frosting into a spiral swirl on top of the last cupcake.

2. Sprinkle with jimmies and place the cupcake in the tray.

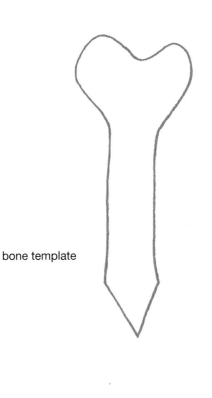

bone template

SPAGHETTI AND MEATBALLS

Drinking milk with spaghetti and meatballs might get you run out of your favorite Italian joint, but when your guests realize this is a platter of cupcakes with frosting pasta and strawberry sauce, everyone will want some. The chunk of Parmesan cheese in the background is actually white chocolate, and best of all, the meatballs are hazelnut chocolates right out of the bag.

10 vanilla cupcakes baked in white paper liners

1 can (16 ounces) vanilla frosting

1/2 teaspoon unsweetened cocoa powder

3 drops yellow food coloring

11 hazelnut chocolates (Ferrero Rocher), unwrapped

3/4 cup low-sugar strawberry preserves (low-sugar has the best color)

2 tablespoons grated white chocolate, plus an additional chunk for garnish

1. Tint the vanilla frosting with the cocoa powder and yellow food coloring and spread a thin layer on top of the cupcakes. Arrange the cupcakes on a serving platter so that they are touching.

2. Spoon the remaining frosting into a ziplock bag. Press out the excess air and seal the bag. Snip a 1/8-inch corner from the bag. Pipe the frosting all over the cupcakes to make the spaghetti, piling it high and allowing some of the spaghetti to hang over the edges.

3. Place the hazelnut chocolates and the strawberry preserves in a medium bowl and toss to coat. Spoon some of the preserves on top of the cupcakes. Place 1 hazelnut chocolate on each cupcake and 1 on the platter. Top the cupcakes

with the remaining strawberry preserves. Sprinkle with the grated white choco-late. Place the chunk of white chocolate on a separate plate with a small hand grater and bring to the table with the platter of spaghetti.

BOX OF CHOCOLATES

This heart-shaped box filled with luscious confections is a selection of mini chocolate cupcakes decorated to look like fancy chocolates. Some of the designs are as easy as using candy hearts and red candy corn. The chocolate truffles are marshmallows dipped in chocolate then drizzled with chocolate. A little deception can be very sweet.

16 mini chocolate cupcakes baked in brown paper liners
(see Sources, page 229)

1 cup plus 2 tablespoons chocolate frosting
2 tablespoons vanilla frosting
1/2 cup chocolate jimmies
3 tablespoons pink, white, and red jimmies
3 tablespoons pink, white, and red nonpareils
(available at baking supply stores or see Sources)
1 cup dark chocolate frosting
4 marshmallows
Assorted Valentine candies (Sweethearts
Conversation Hearts, Valentine candy corn,
marshmallow hearts, Holiday M&M's, heart candies,
foil-covered chocolate hearts, red Dots)

Chocolate box (available at candy counters and party
supply stores or see Sources)

1. Spoon the 2 tablespoons chocolate and vanilla frosting into separate small zip-lock bags, press out the excess air, and seal.

2. Place the jimmies and nonpareils in three separate small shallow bowls. Spread the remaining 1 cup chocolate frosting (not the dark chocolate) on top of 10 of

the cupcakes and smooth. Roll the edges of the cupcakes in the desired sprinkles (see page 12).

3. Spoon the dark chocolate frosting into a 1-cup glass measure. Microwave, stirring frequently, until the frosting is the texture of lightly whipped cream, 10 to 15 seconds. Hold 1 of the remaining 6 cupcakes by its paper bottom and dip the entire top, up to the edge of the paper liner, into the melted frosting. Lift the cupcake straight up and allow the excess frosting to drip off (see page 19). Invert the cupcake and place it on a baking sheet. Roll the edge in the sprinkles, if desired (see page 12). Repeat with the remaining 5 cupcakes.

4. Line a cookie sheet with wax paper. Cut 2 of the marshmallows in half crosswise and 2 in half lengthwise. Using a fork, dip the marshmallow pieces, one at a time, into the remaining dark chocolate frosting to cover (reheat the frosting, if necessary, to maintain the dipping consistency). Allow the excess frosting to drip off. Transfer the coated marshmallows to the cookie sheet and place in the refrigerator for about 10 minutes, until the chocolate has set.

5. Slip an offset spatula or a butter knife under the chilled marshmallows to loosen from the wax paper. Using a toothpick, transfer the marshmallows to the tops of 8 of the chocolate-frosted cupcakes. Snip a $1/16$-inch corner from the bags with the chocolate and vanilla frosting. Pipe swirls or zigzags on top of the marshmallows with the desired frosting.

6. Decorate the remaining cupcakes with the candies. Transfer the cupcakes to the chocolate box. Fill any open spaces in the box with extra candies.

STARRY NIGHT

Van Gogh may have been a little mad, but he wasn't crazy when he created his painterly technique: it hides a lot of mistakes. The canvas for this creation consists of 24 cupcakes; the medium is tinted frosting swirled on using ziplock bags. Since this technique is so forgiving, don't sweat making an exact copy. The final painting should be your own interpretation, not a forgery.

24 chocolate cupcakes baked in gold foil liners (see
     Sources, page 229)

 3 cans (16 ounces each) vanilla frosting (this may seem
     like a lot, but you won't use it all)
     Royal blue, sky blue, golden yellow, moss green, dark
     green, and brown food coloring (available at baking
     supply stores or see Sources)
 8 thin chocolate cookies (Famous Chocolate
     Wafers)
     Empty picture frame, large enough to
     accommodate 24 tightly packed
     cupcakes (optional)

1. Tint the vanilla frosting with the food coloring in the amounts and colors listed below and spoon each color into a separate ziplock bag. Press out the excess air in each bag and seal.

$^1/_4$ cup creamy yellow

$^1/_4$ cup deep golden yellow

$^1/_2$ cup yellow

$^1/_3$ cup light blue

$^3/_4$ cup royal blue

1 cup sky blue

$^1/_2$ cup moss green

$^1/_2$ cup dark green

$^1/_3$ cup greenish brown

2. Place the picture frame, if using, on a board or serving platter. Arrange the cupcakes close together inside the frame opening in 4 rows of 6 cupcakes across or place them directly on a board or serving platter. Using a serrated knife, cut the chocolate cookies into pieces large enough to bridge any gaps between the cupcakes. Snip a $^1/_8$-inch corner from each of the ziplock bags. Pipe some of the sky blue frosting on the cookie pieces and secure them, frosting side down, to the cupcakes.

3. Using the tip of a round toothpick, score an outline of the painting on top of the cupcakes. Pipe outlines of the main subject areas with the appropriate frosting color, such as creamy yellow for the stars, royal blue for the horizon line, dark green for the trees, greenish brown for the grass. Starting from one of the top corners of the cupcake canvas, pipe frosting following the scored outline, blending colors as you go (see page 15) to achieve the desired effect. Continue working your way across the top of the painting, then work your way down to cover the cupcakes completely.

Party Animals

Give a man a fish, and he can eat today. Teach a man to make an aquarium cupcake, and he can party! Making animal cupcakes will get you almost as many hugs as bringing a new pet home to the kids.

MARCH OF THE PENGUINS

Makes 7 penguins,
4 icebergs, and 1 bucket:
12 cupcakes

Penguins are popping up everywhere from Antarctica to Hollywood. And making a penguin cupcake is no more difficult than placing a mini doughnut and a doughnut hole on top of a cupcake. The last penguin home pulls a bucket filled with the catch of the day.

12 vanilla cupcakes, 11 baked in white paper liners and
    1 baked in a silver foil liner

PENGUINS
  4 plain mini doughnuts
  1 can (16 ounces) vanilla frosting
  7 plain doughnut holes
  1 can (16 ounces) dark chocolate frosting
    Black food coloring (available at baking supply
      stores or see Sources, page 229)
  4 marshmallows
  7 thin chocolate cookies (Famous Chocolate Wafers)
  7 yellow fruit chews (Starbursts, Laffy Taffys)
 14 mini chocolate chips

ICEBERGS AND BUCKET
  1 cup shredded coconut
 1/2 cup blue and white rock candy, plus more for garnish
      (available at gourmet candy stores or see Sources)
    Small colored fish candies (available at gourmet
      candy stores or see Sources)
  1 strand black licorice lace

1. Cut the mini doughnuts in half crosswise. Spoon 2 tablespoons of the vanilla frosting into a small ziplock bag, press out the excess air, seal, and set aside. Spread vanilla frosting on 7 of the cupcakes and place a mini doughnut half, cut side down, on top. Spread more vanilla frosting on top of the mini doughnut and place a doughnut hole on top. Spread more vanilla frosting up the sides of the doughnut holes to fill the gap as smoothly as possible (see page 18). Place the cupcakes in the freezer for 10 minutes, until slightly frozen.

2. Tint the dark chocolate frosting black with the food coloring. Microwave in a 1- to 2-cup microwavable measuring cup, stirring frequently, until it is the texture of lightly whipped cream, about 35 seconds total (see page 18). Holding 1 chilled cupcake by its paper bottom, dip it into the black frosting just up to the liner. Hold the cupcake above the surface and allow the excess frosting to drip off (see page 19). Turn right side up and let stand. Repeat with the remaining 6 cupcakes. If the frosting becomes too thick for dipping, reheat for several seconds in the microwave, stirring well.

3. Using clean scissors, cut $1/8$ inch off both flat ends of each marshmallow. Trim $1/4$ inch off one side of 7 of the marshmallow circles to create a straight edge. Press 1 cut marshmallow piece onto the black frosting on each cupcake, straight edge next to the paper liner, to make the penguin's belly.

4. Using a serrated knife, make 2 parallel cuts in each chocolate cookie $1/2$ inch in from opposite sides (see page 20). The 2 curved outside pieces will form the penguin's wings. Trim $1/4$ inch from one end of each wing. Press the trimmed end of the cookie into the frosting just below the penguin's head, one on each side, securing them with a dot of black frosting.

5. Cut 4 of the yellow fruit chews in half on the diagonal to form the triangular beaks. For each penguin, place the cut side of one of the triangles onto the black frosted doughnut hole, pressing gently to secure. Cut and shape the remaining $3 1/2$ fruit chews into fourteen 3-toed feet. Snip a $1/8$-inch corner from the bag with the vanilla frosting. Pipe white dots for the eyes and add the chocolate chips, pointed end in. Pipe a small white highlight on each eye.

1. Spread the remaining vanilla frosting on top of the remaining 5 cupcakes and press the shredded coconut into the frosting. Arrange the rock candy on top of 4 of the cupcakes in the paper liners to make the ice.

2. Add a few fish candies and the licorice lace to the remaining cupcake in the foil liner. Attach the other end of the licorice to one of the penguins to make his catch of the day.

3. Arrange the penguin cupcakes in a curved line on a serving platter. Place 2 fruit-chew feet in front of each penguin. Place the iceberg cupcakes around the penguins and sprinkle the serving platter with fish candy and rock candy. Tuck a fish candy under the wing of one of the penguins.

FAT CATS

These happy cats have dined on white chocolate fish bones. Candy mints form their smooth white cheeks, and soft marshmallow paws hold their frosted tummies.

24 chocolate cupcakes baked in brown paper liners (see
  Sources, page 229)

 2 cans (16 ounces each) vanilla frosting
   Black and orange food coloring (available at baking
    supply stores or see Sources)
 1 can (16 ounces) chocolate frosting
12 thin chocolate cookies (Famous Chocolate Wafers)
24 white mints (Mentos)
12 pink heart candies (Runts)
   Green and brown mini candy-coated chocolates
   (M&M's Minis)
   Black licorice laces
 4 red fruit chews (Starbursts, Jolly Ranchers)
 1 cup white chocolate melting wafers (available at
    baking supply stores or see Sources)
 1 cup mini marshmallows

CAT HEADS

1. Spoon 1 cup of the vanilla frosting into a ziplock bag (for the muzzle). Divide the remaining vanilla frosting into 2 bowls. Tint one bowl of frosting light gray using the black food coloring and one bowl orange (for the fur). Spoon each color into a separate ziplock bag. Tint 3 tablespoons of the chocolate frosting black with the food coloring and spoon into a ziplock bag (for the claws). Spoon the remaining chocolate frosting into a ziplock bag (for the fur). Press out the excess air in the bags and seal.

2. Snip a ⅛-inch corner from the bags of chocolate, gray, orange, and white frostings.

3. Using a serrated knife, make 2 parallel cuts in each chocolate cookie ¾ inch in from opposite sides (see page 20). The 2 curved outside pieces will form the cat's ears. Using the chocolate frosting, attach the ears, cut sides facing each other, to the top of 12 of the cupcakes. Space the ears about 1½ inches apart and allow them to extend 1 inch beyond the edge of the cupcake.

4. Choose your fur color and start by piping several lines of frosting on the ears. For the face, work your way around the edge of the cupcake first, then across, squeezing and releasing the pressure on the bag and pulling the frosting away from the center (see photo, page 15). Leave a wedge shape unfrosted at the bottom for the muzzle. Starting along the bottom edge, pipe white frosting across the wedge-shaped area to cover, allowing the white frosting to overlap the colored frosting.

5. Press 2 white mints into the muzzle, side by side, and place a heart candy above them for the nose. Make the eyes by placing 2 chocolate candies on the colored frosting above the cheeks. Cut small pieces of the black licorice for the eyebrows or closed eyes for the sleeping cats. Cut the red fruit chews in quarters for smaller teardrop tongues and in half for larger tongues, and microwave for a few seconds to soften. Form into small teardrop shapes or 1-inch ovals and attach as the tongue.

BELLIES WITH FISH BONES

1. Place a fish bone template (page 51) on a cookie sheet and cover with wax paper.

2. Place the chocolate melting wafers in a ziplock bag. Do not seal the bag. Microwave for 10 seconds to soften. Massage them and return to the microwave. Repeat the process until the chocolate is smooth, about 45 seconds total (see page 16). Press out the excess air and seal the bag (see page 16).

3. Snip a ⅛-inch corner from the bag and pipe an outline of the fish bone on the wax paper. Fill in the head with chocolate, leaving an opening for the eye. Tap the cookie sheet lightly to smooth the surface. Repeat to make 13 fish bones (the extra one is in case of breakage). Refrigerate until set, about 5 minutes.

4. Pipe frosting fur on the remaining 12 cupcakes, starting around the edges first, then working in concentric circles toward the center, always pulling the frosting away from the cupcake (see page 15).

5. Cut the mini marshmallows in half crosswise. For the paws, press 3 marshmallow halves onto each side of the upper half of the cupcake, cut side in. Snip a $1/16$-inch corner from the bag with the black frosting and pipe and pull black pointed dots on the end of each marshmallow for the claws. Carefully peel the fish bones from the wax paper and arrange on top of the cupcakes.

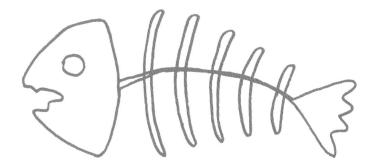

fish bone template

FISHBOWL

Here is a school of low-maintenance pets for the family. Cleaning up after them is so simple: all you need is a fork and a napkin. To make the waterline, the cupcake is double-dipped, first in blue frosting, then in white. Goldfish crackers add a nice salty flavor contrast.

24 chocolate cupcakes baked in dark blue
   paper liners (see Sources, page 229)

 1 can (16 ounces) plus 1 cup vanilla frosting
   Black and blue food coloring
 1 cup praline crunch (Betty Crocker Parlor
   Perfect Ice Cream Topping)
   Green fruit leather
 1 cup goldfish crackers

1. Spoon ⅔ cup of the vanilla frosting into a ziplock bag, press out the excess air, seal the bag, and set aside. Place 2 tablespoons of the vanilla frosting in a small bowl, tint it black with the food coloring, and spoon it into a small ziplock bag. Press out the excess air, seal the bag, and set aside. Spoon ⅔ cup of the vanilla frosting into a small microwavable bowl and cover with plastic wrap. Place the remaining frosting in a medium microwavable bowl, tint it pale blue with the food coloring, and cover with plastic wrap.

2. Place the praline crunch in a shallow bowl. Cut the fruit leather into a variety of leaf shapes from 1 to 1½ inches long. Pinch one end of each leaf to make a seaweed shape.

3. Microwave the blue frosting, stirring frequently, until it is the consistency of lightly whipped cream, 10 to 20 seconds. Working with

one cupcake at a time, dip the top into the blue frosting to cover completely. Allow the excess to drip off (see page 18). While the frosting is still wet, roll one edge of the cupcake in the praline crunch (see page 12). Invert and set aside to dry.

4. Microwave the vanilla frosting in the bowl, stirring frequently, until it is the consistency of lightly whipped cream, 5 to 10 seconds. Dip the edge of each cupcake opposite the crunch topping into the melted vanilla frosting to cover it $3/4$ to 1 inch in from the edge. Allow the excess to drip off, invert, and set aside to dry.

5. Snip a $1/8$-inch corner from the bag with the vanilla frosting. Attach the goldfish and seaweed to the cupcakes with dots of vanilla frosting. Pipe small bubbles of frosting above the fish. Snip a larger corner from the bag and pipe the rim of the fishbowl on the white edge of each cupcake.

6. Snip a $1/16$-inch corner from the bag with the black frosting. Pipe a black eye on each fish. Arrange each cupcake on a small saucer with the praline crunch side down, adding more crunch around the cupcake to help support it.

PANDAMONIUM

PANDAMONIUM

Lazy bears for lazy cupcakers. Oreo cookies do double duty here, forming the arms and legs and crushed into crumbs for the fur.

16 standard vanilla cupcakes baked in white paper liners
16 mini vanilla cupcakes baked in white paper liners

40 chocolate cream-filled sandwich cookies (Oreos)
1 can (16 ounces) plus 1 cup vanilla frosting
Black food coloring (available at baking supply stores or see Sources, page 229)
16 mini marshmallows
32 mini chocolate chips
16 brown chocolate-covered sunflower seeds (available at gourmet candy stores or see Sources)
32 pieces chocolate cereal O's (Oreo O's)
16 green paper liners (optional; available at baking supply stores or see Sources)

1. To make the arms and legs, cut 32 of the cookies in half using a serrated knife and set aside (see page 20). Place the remaining 8 cookies in a food processor and process until finely ground. Transfer the cookie crumbs to a small bowl.

2. Place 2 tablespoons of the vanilla frosting in a small ziplock bag. Tint 1/4 cup of the vanilla frosting black with the food coloring and spoon it into a ziplock bag. Press out the excess air in each bag, seal, and set aside.

3. Using a dot of the remaining vanilla frosting, attach the flat side of 1 marshmallow to the top of each mini cupcake, positioning it on the lower third of the cupcake. Spread the vanilla frosting on top of the mini cupcake, covering the marshmallow to make the muzzle. Smooth the frosting. Snip a 1/16-inch corner from the bag with the black frosting and pipe a mouth just below the muzzle,

with a small vertical line up to the top of the muzzle. Pipe eye patches above and to either side of the muzzle. Add 2 chocolate chips, pointed side in, for the eyes and a sunflower seed for the nose. Press 2 chocolate cereal pieces into the frosting on either side of the top edge of the cupcake to make the ears.

4. Spread the tops of the standard cupcakes with the remaining vanilla frosting, mounding it with your spatula (see page 11). Roll one half of the frosted cupcake into the cookie crumbs to make the black belly fur. Place the mini cupcake heads on their sides on top of the standard cupcakes, lining the faces up with the fur bodies. Snip a $1/8$-inch corner from the bag with the vanilla frosting. Add a dot of frosting where the arms will go and press 2 of the cookie halves, cut side in, on either side of the mini cupcakes to make the arms. Pipe 3 small white lines of frosting on the arms to make the claws. Pipe a small white highlight in each eye.

5. Cut jagged edges on the green paper liners with scissors, if using, and arrange on a serving platter. Set each panda on a green liner. Position the remaining cookie halves, cut side down, next to the pandas to make the legs.

WESTIES

With mini cupcake heads and marshmallow snouts, these dogs are all bite and no bark. Their shaggy coats are made by snipping an M-shaped corner in the ziplock piping bag. To produce the multicolored terriers, you simply use two or three colors of frosting in one bag. When you start squeezing out the frosting, the colors mix at the tip (see page 15).

6 standard vanilla cupcakes baked in white paper
   liners
6 mini vanilla cupcakes baked in white paper liners

1 can (16 ounces) vanilla frosting
   Brown, yellow, and black food coloring (available at
   baking supply stores or see Sources, page 229)
1 cup dark chocolate frosting
12 mini marshmallows
1 tablespoon pink decorating sugar (available at
   baking supply stores or see Sources)
14 black chocolate-covered sunflower seeds (available
   at gourmet candy stores or see Sources)
4 Cinnamon Red Hots
6 strands red licorice laces

1. Spoon ³/₄ cup of the vanilla frosting into a ziplock bag, press out the excess air, and seal. Tint ¹/₄ cup of the vanilla frosting golden brown with the brown and yellow food coloring and spoon it into one side of a ziplock bag. Spoon ¹/₄ cup of the vanilla frosting into the other side of the bag. Spoon 2 tablespoons of the dark chocolate frosting down the center of the bag. Press out the excess air and seal the bag. Tint the remaining dark chocolate frosting black with the food coloring. Spoon ¹/₂ cup of the black frosting into a ziplock bag, press out the excess air, and seal. Spoon 6 tablespoons of the black frosting to one side of a

ziplock bag and spoon the remaining $^1/_2$ cup vanilla frosting to the other side of the bag. Press out the excess air and seal.

2. Cut 6 of the mini marshmallows in half on the diagonal to make the ears and press the cut sides into the pink sugar to coat. Cut the remaining 6 marshmallows on the diagonal to remove one third of the marshmallow. The larger piece will be used to make the muzzle.

3. Reinforce a bottom corner of each ziplock bag with 6 overlapping layers of Scotch tape. Pinch the taped corner flat and snip a small M-shape in the corner (see page 14). First make the head. Working with a different color for each cupcake, pipe a small dot of frosting on the lower half of a mini cupcake, just below the center. Press a large piece of marshmallow, pointed side up, onto the frosting for the muzzle. Pipe two dots of frosting on opposite sides near the top of the cupcake and attach the ears, sugared side up. Pipe several lines of frosting to cover the nonsugared portion of the ears. Then, starting at one ear, pipe $^1/_2$-inch strokes of frosting around the edge of the cupcake, working your way below the muzzle and up to the other ear, always pulling the frosting away from the center. Next, start at the top of the head and pipe long lines, first to the left, then to the right, working your way down to the marshmallow, then covering the sides of the marshmallow. Pipe smaller lines on the front of the marshmallow (leave the marshmallow exposed on the white Westie). Pipe small tufts of hair between the ears. Add 2 of the black sunflower seeds for the eyes and a Red Hot for the nose (use a black sunflower seed for the nose of the white Westie).

4. Now make the body, using one of the standard cupcakes and the frosting that matches the head. Start piping about $^1/_2$ inch in from the edge and work your way around the cupcake. Continue piping rows in concentric circles until the cupcake is covered (see page 15). Turn the decorated head on its side and place on the body. Add a licorice lace for the leash.

5. Continue with the remaining cupcakes, making 2 white Westies, 2 salt-and-pepper terriers, 1 black terrier, and 1 brown mix.

COVER VARIATION

To make the pink tongues, use a pink fruit chew and follow Step 2 for the schnauzer on page 71.

CRAZY HORSES

Whether you're into Mister Ed, Black Beauty, Seabiscuit, or My Friend Flicka, you'll find a creme wafer in a color to match. Customize your horses with frosting and jimmies. You can feed your champions whatever you want, but our ponies like chomping on potato-stick hay.

6 vanilla cupcakes baked in white paper liners

6 chocolate cupcakes baked in brown paper liners (see Sources, page 229)

$^1/_2$ cup chocolate melting wafers (available at baking supply stores or see Sources)

$^1/_2$ cup white chocolate melting wafers (available at baking supply stores or see Sources)

12 chocolate creme wafers (3$^1/_2$ inches long)

12 vanilla creme wafers (3$^1/_2$ inches long)

12 white circus peanuts

2 tablespoons each white, chocolate, and caramel jimmies (available at baking supply stores or see Sources)

1 can (16 ounces) vanilla frosting

1 can (16 ounces) chocolate frosting

6 twist pretzels

Speckled jelly beans and potato sticks for garnish

1. Line a cookie sheet with wax paper. Place the chocolate and white chocolate melting wafers into separate ziplock bags. Do not seal the bags. Microwave for 10 seconds to soften. Massage the chocolates in the bags, return to the microwave, and repeat the process until the chocolate is smooth, about 45 seconds total (see page 16). Press out the excess air and seal the bags.

2. Snip a ⅛-inch corner from each of the bags. Pipe a line of chocolate on one of the flat sides of a chocolate creme wafer. Sandwich another chocolate creme wafer on top and place on the cookie sheet. Repeat with the remaining wafers, using the white chocolate for the vanilla creme wafers. Refrigerate until set, about 5 minutes.

3. For the necks, use a serrated knife to cut diagonally across one end of each pair of creme wafers. For the heads, place the circus peanuts on their sides, flat side facing you, hold your knife at an angle, and cut off a ¾-inch bottom corner. Pipe melted chocolate (either color) on the cut ends of the peanuts. Attach the peanut heads to the cut ends of the creme wafers. Using either color, pipe spots of melted chocolate on one side of the wafers and add jimmies (any color) while the chocolate is still liquid. Refrigerate until set, about 5 minutes. Turn the wafers over, pipe spots of melted chocolate on the other side, and add jimmies. Refrigerate until set, about 5 minutes.

4. Spoon ½ cup each of the vanilla and chocolate frosting into separate ziplock bags, press out the excess air, and seal. Spread the remaining vanilla frosting on top of the vanilla cupcakes and the chocolate frosting on top of the chocolate cupcakes, mounding the frosting slightly in the center (see page 11).

5. Insert a small knife into the top of each cupcake, slightly off to the side. Press 1 creme-wafer neck all the way into the slit in each cupcake at an angle. Snip a ⅛-inch corner from the bags of vanilla and chocolate frosting. Pipe spots on the cupcakes using either frosting. Add jimmies where desired. Pipe ears on top of each peanut head using a dot-and-pull stroke. For the mane, pipe short strokes down the top of the neck by squeezing the bag, then releasing and drawing the frosting away from the neck. Pipe a couple of strokes from between the ears onto the forehead. Pipe chocolate dots for the eyes and nostrils.

6. Using a serrated knife, cut off the 2 rounded sides of each twist pretzel and use the curved pieces for the tails. Insert the tail at the edge of the cupcake. Pipe lines of frosting over the pretzel to cover it.

7. Arrange the horse cupcakes on a platter. Scatter the jelly beans around the cupcakes and stack the potato sticks to make the hay.

PUP CAKES

At the dog park, you know all the dogs but none of the owners' names. Make canine cupcakes and invite the humans to a dog-date. You'll make new friends and maybe snag a few dog sitters too. Details like hair, spots, nose, eyes, and ears give each pup a unique look.

If you choose to make a whole batch of one breed only, just multiply the ingredients for that breed by the number of cupcakes and make only the frosting you need for that breed.

The directions for the breeds begin clockwise starting below the green dog toy.

11 vanilla cupcakes baked in white paper liners

2 cans (16 ounces each) vanilla frosting
1 can (16 ounces) chocolate frosting
1 can (16 ounces) dark chocolate frosting
Yellow, red, brown, and black food coloring (available at baking supply stores or see Sources, page 229)

First, prepare the frosting and be sure to press out the excess air before sealing the ziplock bags. Spoon $1/3$ cup vanilla frosting into a ziplock bag and seal. Tint 1 cup plus 3 tablespoons of the vanilla frosting golden brown with the yellow and brown food coloring. Spoon $3/4$ cup of the golden brown frosting into a ziplock bag and seal. Spoon 3 tablespoons of the golden brown frosting into one side of a ziplock bag and spoon $1/4$ cup of the chocolate frosting into the other side, then seal. Spoon the remaining $1/4$ cup of the golden brown frosting into a small bowl and cover. Tint $1/3$ cup vanilla frosting pinkish brown with the red and brown food coloring. Spoon 2 tablespoons of the pinkish brown frosting into a small ziplock bag and seal. Place the remaining pinkish brown frosting in a small bowl and cover. Tint 1 cup vanilla frosting light gray with the black food coloring. Spoon ¼ cup light gray frosting into a small bowl and cover. Tint the remaining ¾ cup gray frosting a darker shade of gray and spoon half of it into a ziplock bag, then seal. Spoon 3 tablespoons of the remaining dark gray frosting into one side of a ziplock bag and spoon the remaining vanilla frosting (about 3 tablespoons) into the other side, then seal. Tint 1 cup of the dark chocolate frosting black with the black food coloring. Spoon ½ cup of the black frosting into a ziplock bag and seal. Spoon ¼ cup of the chocolate frosting into a ziplock bag and seal. Spoon 2 tablespoons of the dark chocolate frosting into a ziplock bag and seal. Cover any remaining frosting.

YORKSHIRE TERRIER

Makes 1 terrier

1 **thin chocolate cookie (Famous Chocolate Wafers)**
1 **marshmallow**
1 **1-inch piece red fruit leather (Fruit by the Foot)**
1 **pink fruit chew (Starbursts, Tootsie Fruit Rolls)**
1 **brown mini candy-coated chocolate (M&M's Minis)**
2 **brown chocolate-covered sunflower seeds (available at gourmet candy stores or see Sources, page 229)**

1. Using a serrated knife and following the 3 templates, cut the chocolate cookie to make the top of the head and the ears (see page 20). Cut the marshmallow into a ¾-inch cube. Cut the red fruit leather into a ½-inch bow shape. Cut the pink fruit chew in half and form it into a teardrop shape for the tongue.

2. Spread the top of the cupcake with chocolate frosting. Place the large triangle cookie on the top third of the cupcake, pointed end up. Add the small cookie pieces as ears, rounded edge out. Add the marshmallow cube as the snout (see photo, page 75).

Yorkshire terrier templates

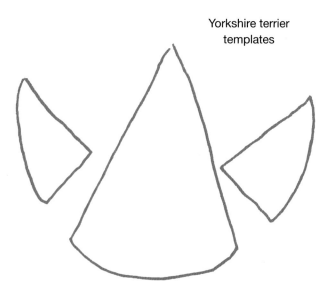

3. Reinforce a bottom corner of the ziplock bag with the golden brown and chocolate frosting using 6 overlapping layers of Scotch tape. Pinch the taped corner flat, then snip a small M-shape in the corner to make a star tip (see page 14). Pipe vertical lines to cover the cookie pieces. Pipe small spikes radiating outward all the way around the edge of the cupcake. Add the pink fruit-chew tongue just below the marshmallow. Starting above the marshmallow, pipe long lines on either side of it. Pipe smaller lines on top of the marshmallow, leaving a V-shape to expose the tongue. Add the brown chocolate candy for the nose, the sunflower seeds for the eyes, and the bow on top.

DALMATIAN

Makes 1 dalmatian

2 **thin chocolate cookies (Famous Chocolate Wafers)**
1 **marshmallow**
2 **mini marshmallows**
1 **pink fruit chew (Starbursts, Tootsie Fruit Rolls)**
2 **brown mini candy-coated chocolates (M&M's Minis)**
1 **small black jelly bean**

1. Using a serrated knife and following the 3 templates, cut the chocolate cookies to make the ears and the mouth (see page 20). Cut the regular marshmallow in half lengthwise.

2. Spread the top of the cupcake with vanilla frosting. Add the mouth-shaped cookie to the lower part of the cupcake. Add 1 marshmallow half, cut side down, and attach the 2 mini marshmallows above the mouth with a dab of vanilla frosting to make the nose (see photo, page 75). Flatten the pink fruit chew to the same size as the cookie mouth and attach it to the mouth with a dot of frosting. Spread vanilla frosting

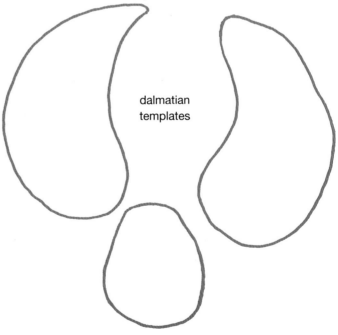

dalmatian templates

on top of the cupcake to cover all but the pink tongue. Snip a ⅛-inch corner from the bag with the vanilla frosting. Pipe a line of frosting around the bottom edge of the mouth.

3. Snip a ⅛-inch corner from the bag with the black frosting. Pipe black spots randomly around the cupcake. Add the brown chocolate candies for the eyes and the jelly bean for the nose. Pipe a white highlight on each eye to add sparkle. Add the cookie ears on either side and press to secure.

COLLIE
Makes 1 collie

1 thin chocolate cookie (Famous Chocolate Wafers)

1 marshmallow

1 small black jelly bean

2 brown chocolate-covered sunflower seeds (available at gourmet candy stores or see Sources, page 229)

1. Using a serrated knife and following the 3 templates, cut the chocolate cookie to make the ears and the ruff (see page 20). Cut the marshmallow in half on the diagonal. Cut the jelly bean in half crosswise.

2. Spread a thin layer of chocolate frosting on top of the cupcake. Press the ears in place, rounded edge in, and add the ruff cookie to the bottom half of the cupcake. Using a dab of frosting, attach 1 marshmallow half, pointed side up, to the top portion of the ruff cookie (see photo, page 75).

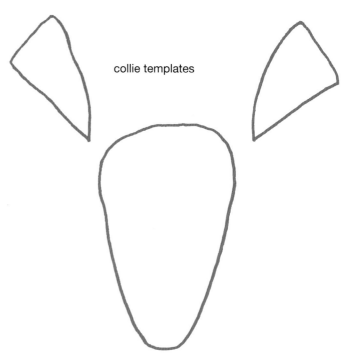

collie templates

3. Snip a ⅛-inch corner from the bags with the chocolate and golden brown frosting. Pipe some of the golden brown frosting over the marshmallow. Spread the frosting to smooth. Pipe the chocolate frosting on the cookie ears, shaping it as in the photo and leaving the center portion unfrosted. Using the fur technique (see page 15),

pipe a $\frac{1}{2}$-inch border of chocolate frosting around the edge of the cupcake, leaving the ruff unfrosted. Pipe a $\frac{1}{4}$-inch border of the golden brown frosting inside the chocolate frosting, overlapping it slightly. Pipe more golden brown frosting to the edge of the cupcake just below the ears. Then pipe the vanilla frosting to make the ruff.

4. Add a jelly bean half to make the nose. Pipe small ovals of vanilla frosting for the eyes and add the sunflower seeds. Pipe a white highlight on each eye and a small line with the golden brown frosting for the mouth.

BEAGLE

Makes 1 beagle

2 thin chocolate cookies (Famous Chocolate Wafers)
1 marshmallow
1 pink circus peanut
2 pieces chocolate taffy (Tootsie Rolls)
1 mini chocolate-covered mint (Junior Mints)
2 brown mini candy-coated chocolates (M&M's Minis)

1. Using a serrated knife and following the 3 templates, cut the chocolate cookies to make the ear supports and the mouth (see page 20). Cut the marshmallow in half on the diagonal. Cut the circus peanut in half, removing the top half, then cut the bottom flat piece in half crosswise (one of these pieces is for the tongue; set the other aside for the chocolate Lab's tongue). Soften the chocolate taffy in the microwave on high for 2 to 3 seconds, then flatten each piece on wax paper with a rolling pin and cut out oval ears large enough to cover the cookie supports.

2. Spread the top of the cupcake with vanilla frosting. Arrange the cookie pieces for the ear supports and mouth on top of the cupcake. Place 1 marshmallow half in the center of the cupcake, large end overlapping the mouth (see photo, page 75).

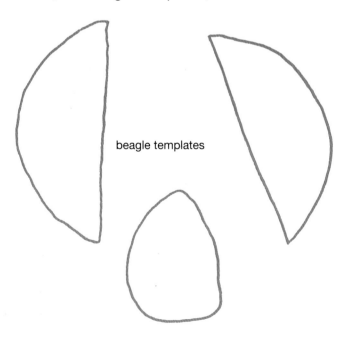

beagle templates

Spread a thin layer of vanilla frosting on top of the marshmallow and the mouth to cover. Press the circus peanut tongue into the frosting on the mouth. Add the chocolate-covered mint to the large end of the marshmallow, just above the tongue, for the nose.

3. Using the bag with the chocolate frosting, pipe freckles on the nose, markings around the eyes, and spikes of hair at the top of the head. Pipe a small spot on each cookie ear support and add the chocolate taffy ears. Pipe 2 dots of vanilla frosting for the eyes and add the brown chocolate candies. Pipe a small white highlight on each eye.

DACHSHUND

Makes 1 dachshund

2 thin chocolate cookies (Famous Chocolate Wafers)
2 brown mini candy-coated chocolates (M&M's Minis)
1 small black jelly bean

1. Using a serrated knife and following the 3 templates, cut the chocolate cookies to make the ears and muzzle (see page 20).

2. Spread the top of the cupcake with black frosting. Place the cookie muzzle on the cupcake, wider end in the center, allowing the cookie to overhang the edge slightly (see photo, page 75). Spread black frosting on the muzzle. Pipe 2 dots of vanilla frosting for the eyes and add the brown chocolate candies. With the golden brown frosting, pipe a line around the edge of the muzzle, fill in the cheek area on either side, and make 2 small ovals above the eyes for the eyebrows. Pipe a small white highlight on each eye.

dachshund templates

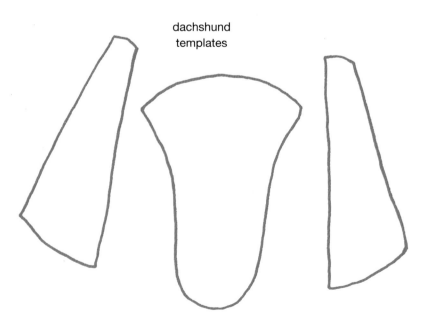

3. Add the cookie ears. Press the jelly bean nose into the golden brown frosting at the end of the muzzle. Pipe several small lines of black frosting at the top of the cupcake for a tuft of hair.

SCHNAUZER
Makes 1 schnauzer

1 marshmallow
1 teaspoon pink decorating sugar (available at baking supply stores or see Sources, page 229)
1 pink fruit chew (Starbursts, Tootsie Fruit Rolls)
2 brown mini candy-coated chocolates (M&M's Minis)
1 small black jelly bean

1. Cut a ¼-inch slice, crosswise, from the end of the marshmallow. Cut the slice into quarters. Press the cut side of 2 of the quartered pieces into the pink sugar to make the ears. Trim away a ¼-inch-wide piece of the rounded side of the remaining large piece of marshmallow (this twice-trimmed piece is the muzzle). Spread the top of the cupcake with a thin layer of the dark gray frosting. Place the marshmallow muzzle on the cupcake, straight side closest to the edge. Arrange the 2 sugared marshmallow ears on either side at the top edge of the cupcake (see photo, page 75).

2. Cut the fruit chew into quarters. Form 1 piece into a teardrop shape for the tongue. Press a knife onto the center of it, lengthwise, to create a crease, and pinch one end.

3. With the vanilla frosting, pipe 2 overlapping rows of small spikes radiating outward on the edge of the cupcake just below the marshmallow. Pipe vertical lines on top of the marshmallow. Snip a ⅛-inch corner from the bag with the dark gray frosting. Pipe a few lines around the edges of the ears and a couple tufts of hair on top. Pipe vertical lines to cover both sides of the marshmallow. Pipe 2 dots of vanilla frosting for the eyes and add the brown chocolate candies. Pipe a small white highlight on each eye. Add the jelly bean nose and the pink fruit-chew tongue.

CHIHUAHUA

Makes 1 Chihuahua

2 thin chocolate cookies (Famous Chocolate Wafers)

1 marshmallow

2 teaspoons white decorating sugar (available at
    baking supply stores or see Sources, page 229)

3 small black jelly beans

1. Using a serrated knife and following the 2 templates, cut the chocolate cookies to make the ears (see page 20). Cut the marshmallow in half crosswise. Spread the top of the cupcake with a thin layer of pinkish brown frosting. Place 1 marshmallow half on the lower half of the cupcake, cut side down, and press into the frosting (see photo, page 75). Spread pinkish brown frosting on the marshmallow to cover.

2. Spread one side of the chocolate cookie ears with the frosting. Sprinkle with the sugar to coat. Press the ears into the cupcake on either side at the top, rounded edge out.

3. Snip a 1/8-inch corner from the bag of pinkish brown frosting and pipe several lines around the edge of the ears. Snip a 1/8-inch corner from the bag with the dark chocolate frosting and pipe a mouth. Press 1 jelly bean on its side into the frosting directly above the mouth to make the nose. Press the 2 remaining jelly beans on end into the frosting for the eyes. Pipe a small white highlight on each eye.

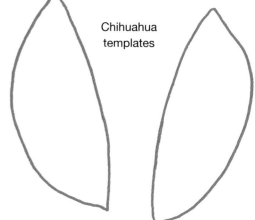

Chihuahua templates

CHOCOLATE LAB

Makes 1 Lab

2 pieces chocolate taffy (Tootsie Rolls)

1/2 pink circus peanut (left over from the beagle)

2 small black jelly beans

3 mini marshmallows

1. Soften the chocolate taffy in the microwave on high for 2 to 3 seconds, then flatten each piece on wax paper with a rolling pin. Cut the taffy with clean scissors to make two 2 1/2-

by-1-inch ovals for the ears. Cut the circus peanut half in half lengthwise. Cut 1 jelly bean in half crosswise.

2. Spread the top of the cupcake with a thin layer of dark chocolate frosting. Arrange the 3 mini marshmallows in a triangle on the lower third of the cupcake (see photo, page 75). Spread a thin layer of dark chocolate frosting over the marshmallows to cover. Place 1 piece of the circus peanut directly under the frosted marshmallows to make the tongue. Pipe lines of dark chocolate frosting around the tongue to cover slightly. With the black frosting, pipe 2 curved lines to define the upper part of the mouth. Press the jelly bean halves into the frosting to make the eyes and add the whole jelly bean on its side for the nose. Pipe a small white highlight on each eye. Fold the top end of the taffy ears under and arrange on either side of the cupcake.

BULLDOG

Makes 1 bulldog

1 **marshmallow**

2 **soft caramels**

1 **piece vanilla taffy (Tootsie Flavor Roll Twisties, Tootsie Roll Midgees)**

1 **teaspoon pink decorating sugar (available at baking supply stores or see Sources, page 229)**

2 **brown mini candy-coated chocolates (M&M's Minis)**

1 **small black jelly bean**

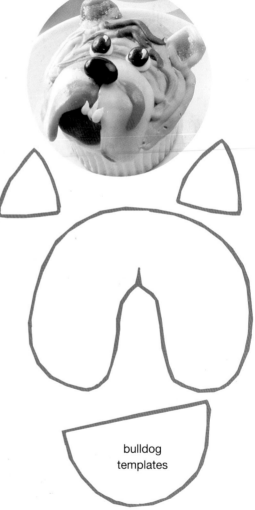

bulldog
templates

1. Cut the marshmallow in half crosswise. Microwave the caramels and the vanilla taffy for 2 to 3 seconds to soften, then knead them together to blend slightly. Roll out the caramel mixture on wax paper to 1/8 inch thick. Using scissors and following the 4 templates, cut the caramel sheet to make the chin, 2 muzzle pieces, and ears. Press one side of the ears into the pink sugar to coat.

2. Spread the top of the cupcake with a thin layer of golden brown frosting. Press 1 marshmallow

half, cut side down, into the frosting on the lower half of the cupcake (see page 75). Pipe lines of golden brown frosting on the cupcake to make the wrinkled skin. Place the caramel chin over the bottom half of the marshmallow. Drape the caramel muzzle piece over the top half of the marshmallow. Bend the caramel ears slightly and insert into the top of the cupcake.

3. Pipe 2 dots of vanilla frosting for the eyes and add the brown chocolate candies. Pipe a small white highlight on each eye. Pipe the teeth with the vanilla frosting. Using a dab of frosting, add the jelly bean on its side for the nose. Using the chocolate frosting, pipe a couple of wavy lines on the forehead for wrinkles and eyebrows.

PUG

Makes 1 pug

1 piece chocolate taffy (Tootsie Roll)
1 pink fruit chew (Starbursts, Tootsie Fruit Rolls)
2 brown mini candy-coated chocolates (M&M's Minis)
1 small black jelly bean

1. Cut the chocolate taffy in half crosswise. Flatten each piece into a 1-inch triangle and bend the pointed end slightly to create the ears. Cut the pink fruit chew in half and flatten to make a 1-inch teardrop shape for the tongue. With a small knife, score a crease lengthwise down the middle on one side and bend the tongue slightly upward, with the scored portion to the outside.

2. Spread the top of the cupcake with the light gray frosting. With the black frosting, pipe an outline of the muzzle on the lower half of the cupcake. Pipe a line inside and adjacent to the outline. Continue piping in this way to fill in the muzzle area. Pipe 2 kidney-shaped outlines for the eyes on either side of the muzzle and fill in with frosting. Pipe a dot on one side of the cupcake for a freckle.

3. Add the brown chocolate candies for the eyes and place the jelly bean on its side for the nose. Press the chocolate taffy ears on either side near the edge at the top of the cupcake. With the dark gray frosting, pipe a few wrinkles between the ears and above the eyes.

4. Insert the tongue in the center of the muzzle, curling upward toward the nose. With the vanilla frosting, pipe small teeth beside and under the tongue. Pipe a small white highlight on each eye.

SHEEPDOG

Makes 1 sheepdog

1 **thin chocolate cookie (Famous Chocolate Wafers)**
1 **marshmallow**
1 **pink fruit chew (Starbursts, Tootsie Fruit Rolls)**
1 **small black jelly bean**

1. Using a serrated knife and following the 2 triangles for the collie ears templates (page 68), cut the chocolate cookie to make the ears (see page 20). Spread the top of the cupcake with a thin layer of light gray frosting. Add the ears, pointed end in, rounded side out, on either side near the edge at the top of the cupcake.

2. Cut a ½-inch slice, crosswise, from the end of the marshmallow. Place the slice flat side down and cut the slice in half crosswise. Place 1 of the marshmallow semicircular slices on the lower half of the cupcake, rounded edge facing the ears (see photo).

3. Cut the pink fruit chew in half and flatten to make a ½-inch teardrop shape for the tongue.

4. Snip a ⅛-inch corner from the bag with the vanilla and dark gray frosting and pipe a row of small spikes below the marshmallow and extending slightly beyond the edge of the cupcake. Place the tongue on the frosting, centering it beneath the marshmallow. Pipe a row of frosting across the bottom half of the marshmallow, overhanging but not covering the tongue. Pipe another row, slightly overlapping the previous row, to cover the marshmallow completely. Pipe slightly longer lines of frosting in the space between the ears, to extend down over the eyes, and cover any other openings on the cupcake. Finish by piping short strokes of frosting on the ears. Add the jelly bean on its side for the nose.

MONARCHS

This swarm of beautiful monarch butterflies is a breathtaking sight. The wings of the butterflies are made using a color-pulling technique blending two colors of candy melting wafers into sophisticated patterns (see sidebar, page 79). By placing the wings in different positions on the cupcakes, you create the illusion of movement and fluttering.

24 chocolate cupcakes baked in brown paper liners (see
   Sources, page 229)

 2 cups dark cocoa melting wafers (available at baking
   supply stores or see Sources)

 2 cups orange candy melting wafers (available at
   baking supply stores or see Sources)

 3 tablespoons white nonpareils (available at baking
   supply stores or see Sources)

$3/4$ cup dark chocolate frosting

 1 can (16 ounces) vanilla frosting
   Yellow food coloring

72 brown candy-coated chocolates (M&M's)

1. Place the 5 templates (page 78) for the wings (2 sizes) and antennae on 2 or 3 cookie sheets lined with wax paper.

2. Place 1 cup each of the dark cocoa and orange candy melting wafers into separate ziplock bags. Do not seal the bags. Microwave for 10 seconds to soften. Massage the wafers in the bags, return to the microwave, and repeat the process until the candy is smooth, about 1 minute total (see page 16). Press out the excess air and seal the bags.

3. Snip a $1/16$-inch corner from each bag. Working on one wing at a time and using the melted dark cocoa, outline the template on wax paper. Go over the outline

several times to thicken. Fill in with the orange melted candy. Tap the pan slightly to flatten. Using a round toothpick, pull the dark cocoa into the orange to create the wing design. While the candy is still liquid, sprinkle the upper portion of the dark cocoa outline with the white nonpareils. Repeat with the remaining melted candy, melting additional wafers as needed, to make 27 pairs of wings (12 small and 15 large sets). Reheat the candy in the microwave for several seconds if it becomes too thick (be careful not to overheat). Place the cookie sheets in the refrigerator until set, about 5 minutes. Follow the same procedure to make the antennae, using the melted dark cocoa.

4. Spoon the chocolate frosting into a ziplock bag, press out the excess air, seal, and set aside. Tint the vanilla frosting pale yellow with the food coloring. Spread the yellow frosting on top of the cupcakes.

5. Carefully peel the chilled wings and antennae from the wax paper. Place 2 brown chocolate candies, $1/2$ inch apart, on top of the cupcakes to form supports for the wings. Press the inside edge of a pair of wings into the frosting about $1/4$ inch apart, allowing the wings to lean on the chocolate candies (some cupcakes can have 2 small butterflies). Gently press the antennae into the frosting at the head of the butterfly. Snip a $1/8$-inch corner from the bag with the chocolate frosting. Starting at the antennae, pipe 4 or 5 beads of frosting down the length of the body, drawing the frosting into a small point on the last bead. Arrange the cupcakes close together on a serving platter.

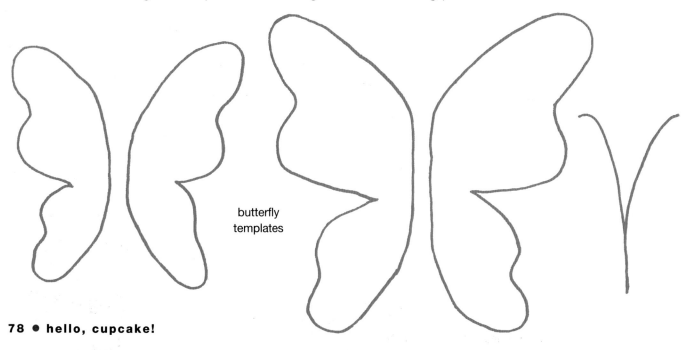

butterfly templates

MAKING PATTERNED BUTTERFLY WINGS

You can make the wings 1 to 2 days in advance and keep them in a cool, dry location.

1. Work quickly because the candy melting wafers will start to set up. Work on one wing at a time. Draw a template on a sheet of paper and cover it with wax paper. Using a ziplock bag filled with melted wafers (see page 16), make an outline of the template in one color. For large designs, pipe around the outline two or three times to get a thick line.

2. Using a second ziplock bag filled with a different color of melted wafers, fill in the inside area.

3. Rap the pan on the surface of the table a couple of times to flatten the melted candy and allow the two colors to smooth into each other.

4. While the candy is still soft, pull a round toothpick through the two colors, from the outside toward the center, to create a pattern.

5. You can add a few sprinkles before the wings set.

SHARK ATTACK!

Yell "Shark!", arm yourself with a fork, and dive right in. In this eat-or-get-eaten cupcake project, the man-eaters boast a Twinkies center, with razor-sharp frosting teeth and a chocolate wafer back fin. The channel markers and chomped-on life preservers are straight out of a scene from *Jaws: The Cupcake Returns.*

11 vanilla cupcakes baked in blue paper liners (see
   Sources, page 229)

2 cans (16 ounces each) vanilla frosting
   Black and blue food coloring (available at baking
   supply stores or see Sources)

Spoon ½ cup of the vanilla frosting into a ziplock bag, press out the excess air, and seal. Spoon ½ cup of the vanilla frosting into a 1-cup glass measuring cup. Tint 1½ cups of the vanilla frosting light gray with the black food coloring and spoon into a 2-cup glass measuring cup or a small glass bowl. Tint 2 table-spoons of the frosting black with the food coloring and spoon it into a small ziplock bag. Press out the excess air and seal the bag. Tint the remaining frost-ing light blue with the food coloring.

FOR THE LIFE PRESERVERS
Makes 3 life-preserver cupcakes

3 plain mini doughnuts
   Red fruit leather (Fruit by the Foot)

1. Place the mini doughnuts on a wire rack over a cookie sheet lined with wax paper.

2. Microwave the vanilla frosting in the 1-cup measuring cup, stirring frequently, until the frosting is the texture of lightly whipped cream, 10 to 20 seconds. Pour

the frosting over the doughnuts to cover completely. Reuse the drippings and reheat if necessary. Refrigerate the doughnuts until set, about 30 minutes.

3. Cut the fruit leather into nine $^1/_8$-by-2$^1/_2$-inch strips. Moisten the back of each strip with a drop of water and wrap 3 strips around each doughnut life preserver as ropes. Use a small fork to remove a bite from the life preserver, if desired.

4. Spread blue frosting on top of 3 of the cupcakes and swirl with the back of a small spoon to create waves. Place 1 life preserver on each cupcake.

FOR THE SHARKS
Makes 3 shark cupcakes

3 cream-filled snack cakes (Twinkies)
2 thin chocolate cookies (Famous Chocolate Wafers)
 Red fruit leather (Fruit by the Foot)
6 mini chocolate chips

1. Place a snack cake on its side, flat side facing you, and holding your knife at an angle, cut 1 inch off the bottom corner. Turn the cake back onto its flat side and trim a small wedge off each side of the uncut end to create a slight V-shape for the shark's snout. Repeat with the remaining 2 cakes. Using a serrated knife, cut the chocolate wafers in half.

2. Spread some of the blue frosting on top of 3 of the cupcakes. Press 1 trimmed snack cake, snout end up, into the frosting on each cupcake. Using a small paring knife, cut a 1-inch slit lengthwise in the lower half of each snack cake (along the shark's spine). Insert 1 chocolate wafer half, flat edge down, 1 inch into the slit to make the fin. Freeze the cupcakes until just firm, 10 to 15 minutes.

3. Cut the red fruit leather into three 1-by-2-inch ovals for the shark mouths and set aside.

4. Microwave the gray frosting in the measuring cup, stirring frequently, until it is the texture of lightly whipped cream, 20 to 30 seconds. Holding a chilled cupcake by the paper liner, dip it into the gray frosting to coat the shark and fin completely. Lift the cupcake above the surface and allow the excess frosting to drip off (see page 19). Turn right side up and let stand. If the frosting begins to

thicken while you're dipping, reheat it in the microwave for several seconds, stirring well.

5. Press the oval-shaped fruit-leather mouth onto the front of the shark's snout. Snip a ⅛-inch corner from the ziplock bag with the vanilla frosting. Pipe the teeth along the top and bottom edge of the fruit leather, pulling each dot of frosting into a point. Press a chocolate chip, flat side up, on each side of the head for the eyes. Snip a ¹⁄₁₆-inch corner from the ziplock bag with the black frosting and pipe 3 gills on each side.

6. Spread blue frosting on each cupcake around the base of the shark and swirl with the back of a small spoon to make waves.

SCHOOL OF FISH
Makes 1 school-of-fish cupcake

1 chocolate-covered marshmallow cookie (Mallomar)

8 red mini gummy fish

1. Spread a small amount of blue frosting on top of the cupcake. Press the marshmallow cookie securely into the frosting, flat side down.

2. Spread more blue frosting on the cupcake and cover the cookie completely. Swirl the frosting with the back of a small spoon to create waves.

3. Press the gummy fish into the frosting, all facing the same direction.

FLOATS

Makes 2 float cupcakes

4 colored spice drops

2 thin pretzel sticks

1. Press the flat sides of 2 different-colored spice drops together. Push the pretzel stick through the center of the stacked spice drops, leaving about 1 inch of the pretzel showing at the top.

2. Spread blue frosting on top of 2 of the cupcakes and swirl with the back of a small spoon to make waves. Insert the longer end of one of the pretzel-stick floats into each cupcake at a slight angle.

CHANNEL MARKERS

Makes 2 channel-marker cupcakes

1 tablespoon light corn syrup

2 mini ice cream cones (Joy Kids Cones)

1 tablespoon each red and green decorating sugar (available at baking supply stores or see Sources, page 229)

2 red mini lollipops (Dum Dum Pops, Tootsie Pops Miniatures)

1. Microwave the corn syrup in a small bowl until bubbly, about 5 seconds. Brush the outside of the mini cones with the hot corn syrup. Sprinkle 1 cone with green sugar to coat and 1 cone with red sugar. Holding the cone upside down, use a round toothpick to make a small hole in the bottom.

2. Unwrap and insert a lollipop into the hole in each cone. Spread blue frosting on top of the cupcakes and swirl with the back of a small spoon to make waves. Press 1 mini cone, lollipop end up, into the frosting on each cupcake. Using the ziplock bag with the vanilla frosting, pipe a number on the side of each cone.

OLD SWAMPY

Old Swampy has just the right balance of fear, fun, and sugar rush. The skin is created using a ziplock bag and a simple frosting technique. If producing the scaly texture scares you more than an alligator does, spread the icing smooth instead.

24 vanilla cupcakes baked in white paper liners

2 cans (16 ounces each) vanilla frosting
Green, yellow, and red food coloring

1 bag (10 ounces) square chocolate alphabet cookies
(Newman's Own)

6 marshmallows

2 mini chocolate-covered mints (Junior Mints)

12 banana-shaped hard candies (Runts)

2 small dark green jelly beans

1. Place 1 tablespoon of the vanilla frosting in a small ziplock bag, press out the excess air, seal, and set aside. Tint the remaining vanilla frosting a murky green (your choice how murky) using the green, yellow, and red food coloring and divide the frosting between 2 ziplock bags. Press out the excess air and seal the bags.

2. Using a serrated knife, cut the cookies in half on the diagonal to make triangles and set aside (see page 20).

3. Arrange the cupcakes on a serving platter in the shape of an alligator (see photo, next page): 2 cupcakes end to end for the snout; 6 rows of 2 cupcakes side by side for the head and body; 6 cupcakes end to end for the tail; and 1 cupcake on each side of the second and fifth rows of double cupcakes for the feet.

4. Snip a ¼-inch corner from each bag of green frosting. Then, starting at the bottom edge of one of the cupcakes and working from one side to the other, pipe

a row of small folds of frosting. Place the tip of the bag on the cupcake, squeeze, and pull about ¼ inch of frosting toward you, then lift the tip slightly and squeeze and fold the ribbon of frosting back onto itself, ending where you started. Pipe 8 or 9 rows, each row moving in the same direction and slightly overlapping the previous row, to cover the top of the cupcake completely. Repeat with the remaining 23 cupcakes.

5. Press 2 of the marshmallows, end to end, into the frosting on the first double set of cupcakes to make the eyes. Pipe green frosting on top of the marshmallows, leaving the outside ends un-frosted, and spread to cover the rounded sides of both marshmallows completely. Using the squeeze-and-fold technique you used on the cupcakes, pipe a decorative line of green frosting around the edge of the unfrosted ends. Snip a ⅛-inch corner from the bag with the vanilla frost-ing. Pipe a spot of vanilla frosting on the flat side of each chocolate-covered mint and attach to the center of the unfrosted marshmallow ends to make the eyes. Pipe a small white highlight on each eye.

6. Arrange the cookie triangles, cut side down, along the cupcakes for the bony plates, keeping them parallel to one another along the back. Add 3 ba-nana candies on each cupcake foot for the claws.

7. Cut each of the remaining 4 marshmallows into 3 triangles to make the teeth. Press 3 teeth into each side of the first 2 cupcakes, pointed ends down. Add the green jelly beans for the nostrils.

Happy Birthday, Cupcake!

Whether you are six going on sixty, or thirty-nine and holding, cupcakes are the best way to say hello to another year. All it takes is a candle to turn them into a birthday celebration. These cupcakes are easy to serve, easy to eat, and no big deal to clean up. And because a standard cake mix makes 24 cupcakes, party planning couldn't be simpler.

WHEN I GROW UP . . .

Changing careers is as easy as switching hats: put on a toque and the chef job is yours; being a cowboy is only a potato chip and a gumdrop away. You can make four of each professional or go on a career hunt and think up some of your own professions. Happy headhunting.

28 vanilla or chocolate cupcakes baked in white paper
   liners

2 cans (16 ounces each) vanilla frosting
   Red, yellow, orange, and black food coloring
   (available at baking supply stores or see Sources,
   page 229)

1 can (16 ounces) chocolate frosting

2 teaspoons instant coffee

1 tablespoon warm water

1. Spoon $1/2$ cup of the vanilla frosting into a ziplock bag, press out the excess air, and seal. Tint $1/4$ cup of the vanilla frosting red, $1/4$ cup yellow, and $1/4$ cup orange with the food coloring. Spoon each into a separate ziplock bag, press out the excess air, and seal. Tint $1/4$ cup of the chocolate frosting black with the food coloring, spoon into a ziplock bag, press out the excess air, and seal. Spoon the remaining chocolate frosting into a ziplock bag, press out the excess air, and seal. Snip a $1/16$-inch corner from each bag and set aside.

2. Dissolve the instant coffee in the warm water. Divide the remaining vanilla frosting into 3 separate bowls. Tint one bowl pale pink with a very small amount of red food coloring, one bowl pale beige with a few drops of the coffee, and one bowl tan with more coffee and a touch of red food coloring. Cover the bowls with plastic wrap to prevent drying.

CHEFS

Makes 4 chef cupcakes

6 marshmallows

4 thin pretzel sticks

8 pieces toasted whole grain oat cereal O's (Cheerios)

4 small pink jelly beans (Jelly Bellys)

8 brown mini candy-coated chocolates (M&M's Minis)

4 red fruit slices

1. To make the 4 chef hats, cut 2 of the marshmallows in half crosswise. Insert a pretzel stick into the center of the cut side of each marshmallow half, pushing it through until 1 inch sticks out the other side. Cut the remaining 4 marshmallows crosswise into thirds. For each hat, arrange 2 of the end pieces, sticky sides down, so that they overlap slightly, and press them on top of the 1 inch of exposed pretzel stick.

2. Spread the top of 4 cupcakes with the pink frosting and smooth. Insert the hat assembly horizontally into one edge of the cupcake. Press 1 piece of cereal into the frosting on either side of the cupcake for the ears. Add a pink jelly bean nose near the center of the cupcake.

3. Pipe vertical lines of vanilla frosting on the base of the marshmallow hat. Pipe white dots for the eyes and add the brown chocolate candies. Pipe a white highlight on each eye. Pipe yellow frosting in curly lines around the top edge of the cupcake, from one ear to the other, to make the hair.

4. Cut the fruit slices into four 1-inch-wide semi-circles and add 1 piece to each cupcake for the mouth.

COWBOYS

Makes 4 cowboy cupcakes

4 shaped potato crisps (Pringles; you may need a few extra in case some break)

4 large yellow gumdrops

4 thin pretzel sticks

8 blue mini candy-coated chocolates (M&M's Minis)

8 pieces toasted whole grain oat cereal O's
   (Cheerios)

4 small cream-speckled jelly beans (Jelly Bellys)
   Red and blue fruit leather (Fruit Roll-Ups)

4 yellow mini candy-coated gum pieces (Chiclets)

1. With the tip of a small knife or a round toothpick, drill a ¼-inch hole in the center of each potato crisp. Press the side of a chopstick into the rounded end of each gumdrop to create a crease in the top of the cowboy hat. Holding the potato crisp with the curved sides pointing up, carefully insert the pretzel stick through the hole in the bottom. Push the pretzel through until about ¼ inch extends out the top of the potato crisp. Insert the ¼-inch length of pretzel into the bottom of the gumdrop.

2. Spread the top of 4 cupcakes with the beige frosting and smooth. Pipe dots of vanilla frosting for the eyes and add the blue chocolate candies. Pipe a white highlight on each eye. Press 1 piece of cereal into the frosting on either side of the cupcake for ears. Pipe chocolate frosting on the top edge of the cup-cake, from one ear to the other, to make the hair. Add a cream-speckled jelly bean for the nose.

3. Cut the red fruit leather into four 1-inch-wide crescent-shaped mouths and four 2½-by-¼-inch strips to use as hatbands. For the bandannas, cut the blue fruit leather into four 1½-by-2½-by-2½-inch triangles and four triangles with each side 1 inch long. Cut a jagged edge on one side of the smaller triangles and pinch together about ¼ inch of the corner opposite the jagged edge.

4. Insert the pretzel end of the hat into the chocolate-frosted edge of the cupcake. Add the red fruit-leather mouth. Pipe a small dot of vanilla frosting on the upper edge of the mouth and attach the yellow piece of gum to make the tooth. Wrap

the red fruit-leather strip around the base of the gumdrop on the hat and secure it with a dot of vanilla frosting. Insert the pinched end of the smaller piece of the bandanna into the cupcake on the left side, just below the ear. Press the remaining piece of the bandanna into the frosting along the bottom edge of the cupcake, allowing it to overhang the side of the cupcake slightly.

BASEBALL PLAYERS

Makes 4 baseball-player cupcakes

- ¹/₄ cup white chocolate melting wafers (available at baking supply stores or see Sources, page 229)
- 4 chocolate-covered marshmallow cookies (Mallomars)
- 4 red and 8 blue mini candy-coated chocolates (M&M's Minis)
- 4 thin pretzel sticks
- 4 small beige jelly beans (Jelly Bellys)
- 4 pink round candies (Mentos)
- 4 pink heart-shaped candies (Runts)
- ¹/₄ cup chocolate cereal O's (Oreo O's)

1. Place the hat brim template on a cookie sheet and cover with wax paper. Place the white chocolate melting wafers in a ziplock bag. Do not seal the bag. Microwave for 10 seconds to soften. Massage the chocolates in the bag and return to the microwave. Repeat the process until the chocolate is smooth, about 25 seconds total (see page 16). Press out the excess air and seal the bag.

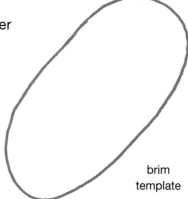

brim template

2. Snip a ¹/₁₆-inch corner from the bag and pipe the outline of the hat brim on the wax paper, then fill in the area with the chocolate. Tap the cookie sheet lightly to smooth the surface. Before the chocolate sets, add the marshmallow cookie to one end of the chocolate hat brim to make the cap. Pipe white lines of chocolate on

the marshmallow cookie for the seams and attach a red chocolate candy at the top. Repeat with the remaining 3 cookies. Transfer the cookie sheet to the refrigerator until set, about 5 minutes.

3. Carefully peel the baseball caps from the wax paper. With the tip of a small knife or a round toothpick, drill a ¼-inch hole through the bottom of the white chocolate into the center of each cookie. Insert ½ inch of a pretzel stick into the cap and set aside.

4. Spread the tops of 4 cupcakes with the tan frosting and smooth. Add a beige jelly bean nose and 2 blue chocolate candies for the eyes. Pipe a white highlight on each eye. Add a pink round candy to one side of the cupcake to make a rosy cheek and a pink heart-shaped candy for the mouth. Insert the pretzel stick end of the baseball cap into the top edge of the cupcake, but do not press the cap flush to the cupcake. For the hair, arrange the chocolate cereal O's around the edge of the top half of the cupcake, pressing them into the frosting and placing a couple of them just under the brim of the cap.

FIREMEN

Makes 4 firemen cupcakes

 1 yellow fruit chew (Starbursts, Airheads, Laffy Taffys)
   Red fruit leather (Fruit by the Foot)
 4 thin pretzel sticks
 4 large red gumdrops
 8 blue candy-coated chocolates (M&M's)
12 small cream-speckled jelly beans (Jelly Bellys)
   Red sprinkles

1. Cut the yellow fruit chew into quarters. Shape each piece into a ¾-inch-wide shield. Cut the red fruit leather into four 2-inch strips and trim one end of each strip to make a rounded edge. Insert a pretzel stick into the center of one of the fruit-leather strips, pushing it through until about ¼ inch extends out the other side. Insert the ¼-inch length of pretzel into the bottom of one of the gumdrops to make the fireman's hat (see photo, page 96). Repeat to make 3 more hats.

2. Spread the tops of 4 cupcakes with the tan frosting and smooth. Add 2 blue chocolate candies to make the eyes and pipe a white highlight on each eye.

Pipe lines of chocolate frosting along the top edge of the cupcake to make the hair. Add a cream-speckled jelly bean on either side of the cupcake to make the ears and 1 on top for the nose. Pipe a line of red frosting for the mouth. Press 3 or 4 red sprinkles into the frosting on one side of the mouth for the freckles.

3. Insert the pretzel stick end of the hat into the center of the chocolate-frosted edge of the cupcake, with the rounded brim to the front. Pipe a small dot of white frosting on the front of the gumdrop and add the yellow fruit-chew shield.

LUMBERJACKS

Makes 4 lumberjack cupcakes

 1 red fruit chew (Starbursts, Jolly Ranchers)
 8 thin pretzel sticks
 2 tablespoons white chocolate melting wafers (available at baking supply stores or see Sources, page 229)
   Red fruit leather (Fruit by the Foot)
 4 large red gumdrops
 4 thin chocolate cookies (Famous Chocolate Wafers)
12 brown mini candy-coated chocolates (M&M's Minis)
 4 small pink jelly beans (Jelly Bellys)

1. Line a cookie sheet with wax paper. Cut the fruit chew in quarters and form each piece into the shape of an ax blade, wider at one end and tapering slightly at the other. Using a serrated knife, cut 4 of the pretzel sticks into 2-inch lengths. Press the cut end of one of the pretzel sticks onto the middle of one side of the ax blade. Place the white chocolate melting wafers in a ziplock bag. Do not seal the bag. Microwave for 10 seconds to soften. Massage the chocolates in the bag and return to the microwave. Repeat the process until the chocolate is smooth, about 25 seconds total (see page 16). Press out the excess air and seal the bag. Snip a $1/8$-inch corner from the bag and pipe a little chocolate over the pretzel end on the fruit-chew ax blade to secure the pretzel stick. Transfer the ax to the cookie sheet. Repeat with the remaining 3 ax blades and refrigerate until set, about 5 minutes.

2. Cut the fruit leather into four 1¼-inch strips and trim one end of each strip into an oval shape for the peak of the cap. Insert one of the remaining 4 pretzel sticks into one of the fruit-leather strips, about ¼ inch from the straight end. Push the pretzel through until about ¼ inch extends out the other side. Push the ¼-inch length of pretzel into the bottom of one of the gumdrops to make the lumberjack's peaked hat. Repeat to make 3 more hats.

3. Microwave the chocolate cookies for about 5 seconds to soften. Use a small paring knife to cut a jagged edge on one side of each chocolate cookie for the beard.

4. Spread the tops of 4 cupcakes with the pink frosting and smooth. Pipe white dots of frosting for the eyes and add 2 brown chocolate candies. Pipe a white highlight on each eye. Pipe wavy lines of orange frosting along the top edge to make the hair. Add a pink jelly bean nose. Press a chocolate cookie beard into the frosting on the lower half of the cupcake. Press the ax, white chocolate side down, into the frosting on one side of the cupcake. Insert the pretzel stick of the hat into the orange frosting. Pipe a black grid of frosting on the gumdrop to make a plaid hat and secure a brown chocolate candy on top. Pipe the eyebrows with the black frosting. Pipe a squiggly red line of frosting on the cookie beard to make the mouth.

OPERA SINGERS
Makes 4 opera-singer cupcakes

½ cup white chocolate melting wafers (available at baking supply stores or see Sources, page 229)

2 red fruit chews (Starbursts, Airheads, Jolly Ranchers)

4 thin pretzel sticks

8 pieces toasted whole grain oat cereal O's (Cheerios)

4 small white jelly beans (Jelly Bellys)

Blue silver dragées (available at baking supply stores or see Sources; optional)

1. Place the hair template on a cookie sheet and cover with wax paper. Place the white chocolate melting wafers in a ziplock bag (see page 16). Do not seal the bag. Microwave for 10 seconds to soften. Massage the chocolates in the bag and return to the microwave. Repeat the process until the chocolate is smooth, about 45 seconds total. Press out the excess air and seal the bag. Snip a $\frac{1}{8}$-inch corner from the bag and pipe the outline of the hair on the wax paper, then fill in with the chocolate (see page 17). Tap the pan lightly to smooth the surface. Transfer the cookie sheet to the refrigerator until the chocolate is set, about 5 minutes.

2. Cut the red fruit chews in half. Shape each half into a $\frac{3}{4}$-inch O-shape for the mouth.

3. Spread the tops of 4 cupcakes with the beige frosting and smooth. Insert a pretzel stick, horizontally, into the top edge of each cupcake, leaving $1\frac{1}{2}$ inches exposed. Carefully peel one of the chocolate hair pieces from the wax paper and press it into the frosting on the top edge of the cupcake, supported by the pretzel stick. Pipe swirled lines of vanilla frosting on top of the chocolate hair as curls. Press 1 piece of cereal into the frosting on either side of the cupcake for the ears. Add a white jelly bean nose. Pipe the closed eyelids with the black frosting. Add a fruit-chew O for the mouth. Press the blue dragées, if using, into the frosting to make a necklace and earrings.

hair template

SAILORS

Makes 4 sailor cupcakes

2 **marshmallows**

Red fruit leather (Fruit by the Foot)

12 **small pink-speckled jelly beans (Jelly Bellys)**

8 **blue mini candy-coated chocolates (M&M's Minis)**

4 **pieces red cereal O's (Fruit Loops)**

1. Cut the marshmallows in half crosswise. Cut the fruit leather into four 1½-by-¼-inch strips and cut a notch in one end of each strip.

2. Spread the tops of 4 cupcakes with the pink frosting and smooth. Pipe lines of chocolate frosting along the top edge of each cupcake to make the hair. Add a pink-speckled jelly bean on either side of the cupcake to make the ears and one on top for the nose. Place a fruit-leather strip on one side of the chocolate hair, notch side down. Add a marshmallow half on top of the hair, cut side down, to make the sailor's cap. Pipe an anchor with the red frosting on the front of the cap.

3. Pipe 2 dots of vanilla frosting for the eyes and add the blue chocolate candies. Pipe a white highlight on each eye. Add 1 red cereal piece to one side to make the mouth.

PARTY PRINCESS

If a princess is pretty in pink, she'll be delicious in pink spice drops. This design is a perfect way to celebrate a special day for your little princess.

12 standard vanilla cupcakes, paper liners removed
12 mini vanilla cupcakes, paper liners removed

24 vanilla wafers
1/4 cup white chocolate melting wafers (available at baking supply stores or see Sources, page 229)
12 thin pretzel sticks
1 cup chocolate frosting
1 can (16 ounces) plus 1 cup vanilla frosting
12 flat whole grain cookies (Peek Freans)
12 pink jelly beans
1/2 cup each white and pink decorating sugar (available at baking supply stores or see Sources)
120 white, red, or pink spice drops
12 thin plain bread sticks
6 yellow fruit chews (Starbursts, Laffy Taffys, Tootsie Fruit Rolls)
12 small red heart decors
Silver dragées (available at baking supply stores or see Sources; optional)

1. Line a cookie sheet with wax paper. Arrange 12 of the vanilla wafers, flat side up, on the cookie sheet.

2. Place the white chocolate melting wafers in a ziplock bag. Do not seal the bag. Microwave for 10 seconds to soften. Massage the chocolates in the bag and return to the microwave. Repeat the process until the chocolate is smooth, about 30 seconds total (see page 16). Press out the excess air and seal the

bag. Snip a ⅛-inch corner from the bag and pipe a dot of chocolate on each of the vanilla wafers. Place the end of a pretzel stick into the chocolate on each wafer, then sandwich together with one of the remaining vanilla wafers, flat sides in. Refrigerate until set, about 5 minutes.

3. Spoon the chocolate frosting and 1½ cups of the vanilla frosting into separate ziplock bags, press out the excess air, and seal.

4. Spread a small amount of the remaining vanilla frosting on top of the standard cupcakes. Place 1 whole grain cookie on top of each cupcake and invert to make the base. Spread a small amount of vanilla frosting on top of each inverted cupcake and add a mini cupcake, top side down (this is the body). Spread a thin layer of vanilla frosting over the stacked cupcakes to cover. Snip a ⅛-inch corner from the bag with the vanilla frosting and pipe a wavy line, about ½ inch wide, along the bottom edge of the cupcake at the base. Cut the jelly beans in half crosswise. Press 2 halves, cut side in and about 1 inch apart, into the frosting at the base of the cupcakes to make the feet.

5. Sprinkle the work surface with the desired color of decorating sugar. Press 10 like-colored spice drops together and roll out with a rolling pin, coating with more sugar as necessary, to make a 6-inch circle about ¹⁄₁₆ inch thick. Repeat with the remaining decorating sugar and spice drops. Use a clean pair of decorative scissors or plain scissors to cut a decorative edge on each circle for the hem. Reroll the scraps with more colored sugar and cut out twenty-four 2-by-2-by-1-inch triangles for the sleeves.

6. Using a round toothpick, poke a small hole in the center of each spice-drop circle. Place 1 circle on top of each set of stacked cupcakes, hole at the top, and make soft folds in the spice-drop gown. Press down slightly to secure. Using a serrated knife, cut a $3/4$-inch length from each end of the bread sticks. You will have 24 pieces. Place a dot of vanilla frosting at the top of each triangle-shaped sleeve and attach to the gown at shoulder level, one on each side, pointed end toward the back. Use a dot of frosting to attach the bread-stick ends under the edge of the sleeves, rounded side out.

7. Pipe a wavy edge of vanilla frosting around the top of the gown for the collar and on the edge of each sleeve. Insert a pretzel and vanilla cookie combo through the hole in the top of the gown and into the cupcake, leaving $1/4$ inch of the pretzel exposed to make the neck.

8. Cut the yellow fruit chews in half and roll each piece into a 2-by-$3/4$-inch strip. Cut a jagged edge along one length of the strip and press the short ends together to form the crown. Snip a $1/16$-inch corner from the bag with the chocolate frosting. Pipe curly hair and 2 small dots for eyes on the vanilla wafer. Place the crown on top of the hair. Pipe a small dot of vanilla frosting on the face for the mouth and add the heart decor. Pipe vanilla frosting dots on the crown and press a silver dragée, if using, into each dot.

SLUMBER PARTY

A slumber party is a dream for the kids but can be a nightmare for the parents. The drowsy tots on board these cupcakes may be the only ones sleeping, so serve with glasses of warm milk to ease the party into dreamland.

6 vanilla cupcakes baked in white paper liners

1 can (16 ounces) vanilla frosting
   Orange, yellow, and green food coloring (available at
   baking supply stores or see Sources, page 229)
1/2 cup chocolate frosting
6 marshmallows
2 small pink jelly beans (Jelly Bellys)
2 each light pink, dark pink, yellow, orange, blue,
   purple, and green fruit chews (Starbursts, Laffy
   Taffys, Airheads)
6 mini vanilla wafers
   Pink and red heart decors
2 bear-shaped graham crackers (Teddy Grahams)
   Red sprinkles

1. Spoon 2 tablespoons of the vanilla frosting into a small ziplock bag, press out the excess air, and seal. Tint 2 tablespoons of the vanilla frosting each with the orange, yellow, and green food coloring and spoon into separate small ziplock bags. Press out the excess air and seal the bags. Place the chocolate frosting in a ziplock bag, press out the excess air and seal.

2. Spread the top of the cupcakes with the remaining 1 1/2 cups vanilla frosting and smooth. Cut the marshmallows in half lengthwise. Place 1 marshmallow piece, lengthwise and cut side down, on the lower half of one of the cupcakes. Place

another marshmallow piece crosswise, cut side down, near the top edge of the cupcake to make the pillow. Repeat with the remaining 5 cupcakes. On one of the cupcakes, press the jelly beans into the frosting at the bottom edge, just below the end of the marshmallow, to make the feet.

3. Working with 2 like-colored fruit chews at a time, heat them in the microwave for 2 to 3 seconds to soften. Press the fruit chews together and roll out on a sheet of wax paper to $^1/_{16}$ inch thick. Cut a 2-inch square from all but the purple fruit-chew piece and a 2-by-$^1/_2$-inch strip from the scraps. Using craft scissors with a decorative edge, cut along one side of each strip to make a zigzag blanket edge. Press contrasting colors of fruit-chew squares and strips together to make the blankets with borders. Cut a $^3/_4$-by-$1^1/_2$-inch rectangle from the rolled-out purple fruit-chew piece. Cut a $^3/_4$-inch square from the scraps of the yellow fruit chews and place on one side of the purple fruit chew. Fold the purple fruit chew over the yellow to make a book.

4. Snip a $1/16$-inch corner from each of the 5 bags with the frostings. Pipe a dot of frosting on the marshmallow pillow and add the vanilla wafer, flat side down. Using the orange, yellow, or chocolate frosting, pipe hair along the top edge of each wafer. Pipe the children's eyelids or eyebrows with chocolate frosting and the eyes with a dot of vanilla frosting, then a dot of chocolate. Pipe a dot of vanilla frosting for the mouths and add the pink or red heart decors. Pipe the teddy bear's eyes and mouth with chocolate frosting. Pipe a tiny dot of vanilla

frosting for the bear's nose and add a red sprinkle. On the cover of the book, pipe a ghost with vanilla frosting and writing with chocolate frosting.

5. Press the blankets over the marshmallow bodies and pipe decorations on top with the colored frosting. Attach the teddy bear cookies and the book with a dot of frosting.

BIG BIRTHDAY CAKE

Each tier of this fancy birthday cake is decorated with a different candy in a color to match the paper liners. Because they are stacked on frosted cupcakes, the liners are gooey. If you prefer a neater party, use a tiered cake stand (available from home decorating stores or see Sources, page 229). If tradition calls for blowing out candles, just add a few real ones among the faux.

17 vanilla cupcakes baked in purple paper liners (see Sources)

8 vanilla cupcakes baked in orange paper liners (see Sources)

5 vanilla cupcakes baked in blue paper liners (see Sources)

3 vanilla cupcakes baked in yellow paper liners

1 vanilla cupcake baked in a pink paper liner (see Sources)

2 cans (16 ounces each) vanilla frosting
Orange food coloring (available at baking supply stores or see Sources)
Hard candies in colors to match the paper liners (blue flowers, pink hearts; Runts)

17 strawberry Pirouette cookies

17 thin pretzel sticks
Chocolate-covered sunflower seeds in colors to match the paper liners (available at gourmet candy stores or see Sources)

17 banana-shaped hard candies (Runts)

1. Tint ¼ cup of the vanilla frosting orange with the food coloring and spoon it into a ziplock bag. Press out the excess air, seal the bag, and set aside.

2. Separate the candies into like colors in small bowls.

3. Working on one tier at a time and starting with the 17 cupcakes in purple paper liners, spread the vanilla frosting on top of the cupcakes and smooth. Arrange the cupcakes in a circle on a flat serving platter (6 cupcakes in the center surrounded by 11 cupcakes). Press the purple candies into the frosting on the outer edge of the cupcake circle.

4. Continue with the next tier of 8 cupcakes in orange paper liners (1 cupcake in the center surrounded by 7 cupcakes) and press the orange candies into the frosting on the outer edge of the cupcake circle. Follow the same technique with the 5 cupcakes in blue paper liners, the 3 cupcakes in yellow paper liners, and, finally, the cupcake in the pink paper liner, pressing the color-coordinated candies into the outer edge of the cupcakes.

5. Cut the Pirouette cookies into seventeen 3-inch pieces. Insert 1 pretzel stick into each cookie piece, leaving 1 inch of the pretzel exposed. Press the cookie, pretzel stick down, into the center of 13 evenly spaced cupcakes on the bottom 3 tiers and into each of the cupcakes in the top 2 tiers to form the candles.

6. Arrange the chocolate-covered sunflower seeds, in colors that match the paper liners, around the base of each cookie candle in a radiating flower pattern (use tweezers to place the small candies).

7. Snip a ⅛-inch corner from the bag with the orange frosting and pipe a small dot of frosting on top of each cookie candle. Press a banana-shaped candy into each cookie top. Pipe a line of orange frosting around the banana candy to make the flame.

BOWL ME OVER

Makes 10 bowling pins
and 1 bowling ball:
11 cupcakes

You'll be sure to score a strike when you serve these bowling party cupcakes that look so much like the real deal that you may have to give them a squeeze just to make sure you can eat them. The pins are created by building up the shape on top of the cupcake, then dipping it in melted frosting to form a smooth outer coating. They're a great dessert for your birthday bowling buddies before, during, or after a game.

10 standard vanilla cupcakes baked in white paper
   liners
1 standard vanilla cupcake baked in a brown paper
   liner (see Sources, page 229)
10 mini vanilla cupcakes, paper liners removed

1 can (16 ounces) plus 1 cup vanilla frosting
10 plain doughnut holes
   Red fruit leather (Fruit by the Foot)
2 tablespoons black decorating sugar (available at
   baking supply stores or see Sources)
3 tablespoons chocolate frosting
3 large chocolate chips (Hershey's Mini Kisses)

1. Spoon 2 tablespoons of the vanilla frosting into a small ziplock bag, press out the excess air, seal, and set aside. Spread vanilla frosting on top of the 10 standard cupcakes in white paper liners, mounding it slightly (see page 11). Place one of the mini cupcakes, top side down, on top of each cupcake. Spread a little frosting on top of the mini cupcake and add a doughnut hole. Spread frosting up the sides of the mini cupcake and doughnut to fill the gaps and make as smooth as possible (see photo, page 18). Place the cupcakes in the freezer for 10 to 15 minutes, until slightly frozen.

2. Spoon the remaining vanilla frosting into a 2-cup microwavable measuring cup. Microwave, stirring frequently, until the frosting is the texture of lightly whipped cream, 30 to 35 seconds total. Working with one cupcake at a time, hold the chilled cupcake by the paper liner and dip it into the melted frosting up to the edge of the paper liner. Lift the cupcake above the surface and allow the excess frosting to drip back into the cup (see page 19). Turn upright and let stand to set. If the frosting becomes too thick to dip, reheat in the microwave for several seconds, stirring well.

3. Cut the fruit leather into twenty $5\frac{1}{2}$-by-$\frac{1}{8}$-inch strips and ten 1-by-$\frac{3}{4}$-by-$\frac{3}{4}$-inch triangles. Snip a $\frac{1}{8}$-inch corner from the bag with the vanilla frosting. Pipe dots of frosting on the dipped cupcakes and attach the pieces of fruit leather, as shown, to make the pin markings.

4. To make the bowling ball, place the black decorating sugar in a small shallow bowl. Spread the chocolate frosting on top of the cupcake in the brown paper liner, mounding it slightly. Starting on the edge, roll the top of the cupcake in the black sugar to cover. Press the chocolate chips, pointed side down, into the cupcake to make the finger holes.

5. Arrange the bowling pin cupcakes on a wooden serving tray or cutting board in a triangular configuration to look like the pins at a bowling alley and place the ball cupcake beside them.

THE BIG TOP

Forget hiring the clown and rounding up a trick pony for the party. Invest your effort in this super birthday project that will make all the other kids want to call you Mom. This is one of our most adventurous projects, but each cupcake design is fairly easy to make. Special birthdays call for love and dedication, so roll up your sleeves and start making monkeys.

25 standard vanilla cupcakes baked in white
　　paper liners
　4 mini vanilla cupcakes, paper liners removed

　2 cans (16 ounces each) plus 1 cup vanilla frosting
　　Yellow, orange, blue, and red food coloring (available
　　at baking supply stores or see Sources, page 229)
$3/4$ cup chocolate frosting
　9 striped paper cupcake liners (available at baking
　　supply stores or see Sources)
　　Thin orange ribbon, cut into three 12-inch lengths
　　A 4-tiered serving platter (available at home
　　decorating stores or see Sources)

Tint 1 cup of the vanilla frosting bright yellow with the food coloring. Tint 1 cup of the vanilla frosting orange with the food coloring and spoon $1/2$ cup into a ziplock bag. Press out the excess air and seal the bag. Reinforce a bottom corner of the ziplock bag with the orange frosting using 6 overlapping layers of Scotch tape (see page 13). Tint $1/2$ cup of the vanilla frosting light blue with the food coloring. Tint 2 tablespoons of the vanilla frosting light pink with the food coloring and spoon into a small ziplock bag. Press out the excess air and seal the bag. Tint 2 tablespoons of the vanilla frosting red with the food coloring and spoon into a small ziplock bag. Press out the excess air and seal the bag. Spoon $1/4$ cup of the vanilla frosting into a ziplock bag, press out the excess air,

and seal the bag. Spoon the remaining 1 cup vanilla frosting into a bowl. Spoon ¼ cup of the chocolate frosting into a ziplock bag, press out the excess air, and seal.

TOPPER

Makes 1 cupcake

1 orange-striped candy stick, about 4 inches long

1 orange and vanilla fruit chew (Creme Savers Soft Candy)

1 small green gummy ring (LifeSavers Gummies)

3 tablespoons small round candies

1. Spread the top of 1 of the standard cupcakes with vanilla frosting and smooth. Place the cupcake inside a striped paper liner. Insert the candy stick upright into the center of the cupcake. Roll out the fruit chew on a sheet of wax paper to ⅛ inch thick. Using a small cookie cutter or clean scissors, cut out a 1½-inch-wide flower shape.

2. Snip a ¹⁄₁₆-inch corner from the bag with the vanilla frosting. Pipe a small dot of frosting on top of the candy stick. Add the gummy ring and press the ends of the three 12-inch ribbons into the frosting to secure. Place the flower-shaped fruit chew on top of the gummy ring. Pipe a dot of frosting in the center of the fruit chew and add 1 round candy. Arrange the remaining candies around the base of the candy stick to cover the top of the cupcake. Place on the top tier of the serving platter.

POODLES

Makes 4 poodle cupcakes

½ cup white nonpareils (available at baking supply stores or see Sources, page 229)

8 marshmallows

8 brown chocolate-covered sunflower seeds (available at gourmet candy stores or see Sources)

4 red mini candies (M&M's Minis or Cinnamon Red Hots)

Large peppermint balls, unwrapped

1. Place the nonpareils in a small shallow bowl. Spread the tops of 4 of the standard cupcakes and the 4 mini cupcakes with vanilla frosting. Roll the edges of the cupcakes in the nonpareils to coat (see page 12).

2. Using clean scissors, cut 4 of the marshmallows in half on the diagonal. Cut 4 of the halved pieces in half again, lengthwise, to make the ears. Press the ear pieces, cut side in, on either side of the top of each mini cupcake. Trim the remaining marshmallow halves to make four $^3/_4$-inch-long cone shapes. Press one of the marshmallow cones, narrowed end up, into the frosting in the center of each mini cupcake to make the muzzle. Cut small pieces from the remaining 4 marshmallows and arrange at the top of each mini cupcake to make little tufts of hair. Insert 2 of the sunflower seeds above the muzzle for the eyes. Pipe a small dot of vanilla frosting on top of the muzzle and add a red candy nose.

3. Place one of the mini cupcakes on its side on top of each of the 4 standard cupcakes. Arrange on the third tier of the serving platter with peppermint balls between the cupcakes.

CLOWNS
Makes 8 clown cupcakes

$^1/_4$ cup white chocolate melting wafers (available at baking supply stores or see Sources, page 229)

16 vanilla wafers

8 thin pretzel sticks

2 tablespoons each pink, yellow, blue, and green decorating sugars (available at baking supply stores or see Sources)

8 corn-chip cone snacks (Bugles)

1 roll red fruit leather (Fruit by the Foot)

16 brown chocolate-covered sunflower seeds (available at gourmet candy stores or see Sources)

$^1/_4$ cup multicolored plus 8 red mini candy-coated chocolates (M&M's Minis)

$^1/_2$ cup rainbow nonpareils (available at baking supply stores or see Sources)

8 orange and vanilla fruit chews (Creme Savers Soft Candy)

8 small green gummy rings (LifeSavers Gummies)
8 orange circus peanuts

1. Line a cookie sheet with wax paper. Place the white chocolate melting wafers in a ziplock bag. Do not seal the bag. Microwave for 10 seconds to soften. Massage the chocolates in the bag and return to the microwave. Repeat the process until the chocolate is smooth, about 30 seconds total (see page 16). Press out the excess air and seal the bag.

2. Snip a $1/8$-inch corner from the bag. Place 8 of the vanilla wafers, flat side up, on the cookie sheet and pipe a dot of melted chocolate on each. Lay the end of a pretzel stick in the chocolate on each wafer, then sandwich together with one of the remaining vanilla wafers, flat side in, to make the heads and necks (see photo, page 102). Refrigerate until set, about 5 minutes.

3. Place each of the colored decorating sugars in a separate small shallow bowl. For the clown hats, pipe melted chocolate over the corn-chip cones, spread to coat and, while still wet, roll the cones in the colored sugars to coat, making 2 of each color. Transfer the sugared hats to the cookie sheet and refrigerate until set, about 5 minutes.

4. Cut the red fruit leather into eight $3/4$-inch-wide boomerang shapes to make the mouth. Working on one clown face at a time, pipe several dots of vanilla frosting on one side of the sandwiched vanilla wafers in the mouth position and attach a fruit-leather mouth. Pipe 2 dots of vanilla frosting for the eyes and attach 2 sunflower seeds. Pipe a dot of vanilla frosting for the nose and attach a red mini candy-coated chocolate. Pipe a line of vanilla frosting on the mouth.

5. Place the rainbow nonpareils in a small shallow bowl. Spread the tops of 8 of the standard cupcakes with yellow frosting and smooth. Roll the edges of the cupcakes in the nonpareils (see page 12). Place each of the cupcakes inside a striped paper liner. Roll out each orange and vanilla fruit chew on a sheet of wax paper to $1/8$ inch thick. Using a small cookie cutter or clean scissors, cut a $1^1/2$-inch-wide flower shape from each flattened fruit chew. With a round toothpick, poke a hole in the center of the fruit chews large enough for the pretzel stick to go through.

6. Place a gummy ring on top of each cupcake. Lay a flower-shaped fruit chew on

top of the gummy ring and insert the pretzel-stick neck into the hole in the fruit chew, through the center of the gummy ring and into the cupcake.

7. Pinch the taped corner of the ziplock bag with the orange frosting flat, then snip a small M-shape in the corner to make a star tip (see page 14). Pipe the hair with the orange frosting, making small star shapes along the edge of the vanilla wafer. Press a sugared hat into the orange-frosting hair. Press 2 like-colored mini candy-coated chocolates into the yellow frosting on the cupcake for the buttons. Place the clown cupcakes on the second tier of the serving platter. Cut the circus peanuts in half crosswise and arrange them in front of the cupcakes to make the feet.

ELEPHANTS

Makes 4 elephant cupcakes

1 cup light blue candy melting wafers (available at baking supply stores or see Sources, page 229)

¼ cup light blue decorating sugar (available at baking supply stores or see Sources)

8 banana-shaped hard candies (Runts)

8 brown mini candy-coated chocolates (M&M's Minis)

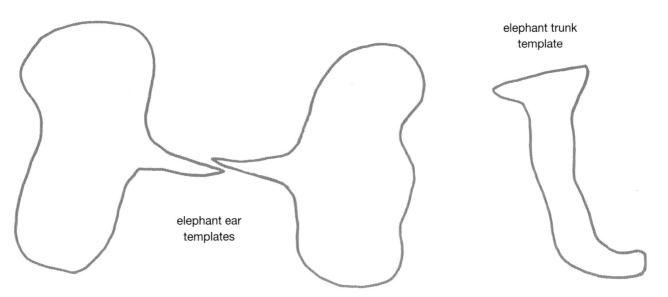

1. Place the ear templates on a cookie sheet and cover with wax paper. Place the trunk template on a separate cookie sheet and cover with wax paper. Place the light blue candy melting wafers in a ziplock

elephant trunk template

elephant ear templates

bag. Do not seal the bag. Microwave the wafers for 10 seconds to soften. Massage the mixture in the bag, return to the microwave, and repeat the process until the candy is smooth, about 30 seconds total (see page 16). Press out the excess air and seal the bag.

2. Snip a 1/8-inch corner from the bag. Pipe an outline of the ears on the wax paper, then fill in with the melted candy (see page 17). Tap the sheet lightly to flatten the candy. Place small balls of aluminum foil under the wax paper beneath the ears before they set (this gives the ears a little movement). Refrigerate until set, about 5 minutes. Working with the trunk template, pipe a very tight pattern of zigzag lines with the melted candy to make the trunk. Do not tap the cookie sheet to flatten. Place the cookie sheet in the refrigerator until set, about 5 minutes.

3. Place the blue decorating sugar in a small shallow bowl. Spread the tops of 4 of the standard cupcakes with the blue frosting and smooth. Roll the edges of the cupcakes in the sugar (see page 12). Carefully peel the ears and trunks from the wax paper. Insert the ears into either side of each cupcake. Press the trunk into the center of the cupcake. Press a banana candy into the frosting on either side of the trunk for the tusks. Pipe 2 dots of vanilla frosting for the eyes and add the brown chocolate candies. Pipe a white highlight on each eye. Pipe lines of vanilla frosting on the ears and 2 dots on the end of the trunk for the nostrils. Refrigerate the cupcakes for about 30 minutes to help secure the ears. Arrange the elephant cupcakes on their sides on the first tier of the serving platter along with the monkey and lion cupcakes.

MONKEYS

Makes 4 monkey cupcakes

1/2 cup chocolate jimmies

8 chocolate cereal O's (Oreo O's)

8 brown mini candy-coated chocolates (M&M's Minis)

8 purple chocolate-covered sunflower seeds (available at gourmet candy stores or see Sources, page 229)

1. Place the chocolate jimmies in a small shallow bowl. Spread the tops of 4 of the standard cupcakes with chocolate frosting and smooth. Roll the edges of the top

half of the cupcakes in the jimmies (see page 12). Add 2 chocolate cereal O's on either side of the cupcakes for the ears.

2. Snip a ⅛-inch corner from the bags with the pink and red frosting. Pipe a 2-inch pink horizontal oval on the lower third of each cupcake to make the muzzle. Pipe 2 small vanilla vertical ovals directly above the pink oval and add the brown chocolate candies for the eyes. Pipe a white highlight on each eye. Place 2 sunflower seeds, vertically, on the pink muzzle for the nose. Pipe a mouth with the red frosting. Add 1 jimmy above each eye for the eyebrows. Arrange the monkey cupcakes on their sides on the first tier of the serving platter along with the elephant and lion cupcakes.

LIONS

Makes 4 lion cupcakes

Red licorice laces (Twizzlers Pull-n-Peel)
8 orange cereal O's (Fruit Loops, Apple Jacks)
8 blue mini candy-coated chocolates (M&M's Minis)
4 small pink heart-shaped hard candies (Runts)

Cut the licorice laces into ¾-inch lengths. Spread the tops of the remaining 4 standard cupcakes with the orange frosting and smooth. To make the lion's mane, press the licorice pieces into the frosting around the outside edge of the cupcake, creating a small V-shaped hairline at the top. Add the orange cereal O's on either side of the cupcake to make the ears. Add the blue chocolate candies for the eyes. Pipe a white highlight on each eye. Place the heart-shaped candy in the center for the nose. Snip a ⅟₁₆-inch corner from the bag with the chocolate frosting and pipe the mouth (2 adjoining semicircles) and whisker holes. Arrange the lion cupcakes on their sides on the first tier of the serving platter along with the elephant and monkey cupcakes.

Hostess with the Mostest

When you've got a reason to celebrate, bring out the wow in the occasion with cupcakes. Baby showers, family reunions, summer garden parties—even weddings— are all great opportunities to show off your cupcaking prowess.

SUNFLOWERS

The petals on these bright, sassy cupcakes may look complicated but are actually quick and easy: just grab a ziplock bag filled with 2 colors of frosting and squeeze, pull, and release. Practice makes perfect.

24 vanilla cupcakes baked in green paper liners (see Sources, page 229)

2 cans (16 ounces each) vanilla frosting
Green, yellow, orange, and black food coloring (available at baking supply stores or see Sources)

14–16 regular chocolate cream-filled sandwich cookies (Oreos)

25–30 mini chocolate cream-filled sandwich cookies (Mini Oreos)

$1/2$ cup table sugar

15–20 candy spearmint leaves or 2 rolls green fruit leather

2 tablespoons dark chocolate frosting

6–10 red candy-coated chocolates (M&M's)

Basket lined with green tissue paper (optional)

1. Tint $1^1/2$ cups of the vanilla frosting green with the food coloring. Spread an even layer of the green frosting on top of the cupcakes and smooth. Arrange the chocolate sandwich cookies, regular and mini, randomly over the cupcakes, pressing them into the frosting to secure.

2. Tint the remaining vanilla frosting bright yellow with the food coloring. Remove $1/2$ cup of the yellow frosting and tint it orange with the food coloring. Spoon $1/4$ cup of the orange frosting into one side of a ziplock bag and spoon half of the yellow frosting into the other side of the bag. Press out the excess air and seal the bag. Repeat the process with another ziplock bag and the remaining orange and yellow frosting. Reinforce the corner of each bag with 6 overlapping layers

of Scotch tape. Pinch the taped corners flat and cut a small V-shape in the corner to make a leaf tip. Pipe yellow-orange frosting around the edge of each cookie to make petals (see page 14). Pipe another circle of petals just inside the first and slightly overlapping.

3. Sprinkle the work surface with the sugar. Roll out the spearmint leaves, one at a time, to ⅛ inch thick. Using clean scissors, cut the candies or fruit leathers into 1½-inch-long leaf shapes. Press the leaves into the cupcakes just under the petals.

4. Tint the chocolate frosting black with the food coloring and spoon it into a small ziplock bag. Press out the excess air and seal the bag. Snip a ¹⁄₁₆-inch corner from the bag. Pipe a dot of black frosting on some of the cookies and attach the red chocolate candies to make the ladybugs. Pipe a line of black frosting down the center of each ladybug and add a dot for the head and a few dots on the back.

5. Arrange the cupcakes close together in a basket lined with green tissue paper, if you like, in small cups or on a platter.

BLACK AND WHITE PARTY

These patterns are as sophisticated as Truman Capote's celebrated Black and White Ball. And just as with any fancy dress event, it is what's on the outside that counts. Tinting dark chocolate frosting with black food coloring makes the deep black color; the white frosting is straight out of the can.

10 chocolate cupcakes baked in white paper liners

1/4 cup dark cocoa melting wafers (available at baking supply stores or see Sources, page 229)

3 tablespoons each black and white nonpareils (available at baking supply stores or see Sources)

3 tablespoons each black and white decorating sugars (available at baking supply stores or see Sources)

3 tablespoons black jimmies (available at baking supply stores or see Sources)

1 cup dark chocolate frosting
Black food coloring (available at baking supply stores or see Sources)

1 cup vanilla frosting

1 tube black decorating gel
Assorted black and white candies and cookies, such as:
    Black licorice gumdrops (Crows)
    Black and white chocolate-covered sunflower seeds (available at gourmet candy stores or see Sources)
    Black and white Licorice Pastels
    White candy-coated chocolates (M&M's)
    Thin chocolate cookies (Famous Chocolate Wafers), cut into small wedges with a serrated knife (see page 20)

1. Line a cookie sheet with wax paper. Place the dark cocoa melting wafers in a ziplock bag. Do not seal the bag. Microwave for 10 seconds to soften. Massage the chocolate in the bag, return to the microwave, and repeat the process until the chocolate is smooth, about 30 seconds total (see page 16). Press out the excess air and seal the bag.

2. Snip a ⅛-inch corner from the bag. Pipe ¼-inch and ½-inch dots on the wax paper. While the chocolate is still wet, sprinkle the top of the dots with the white or black nonpareils to cover them completely. Refrigerate until set, about 5 minutes. Peel the chocolates from the wax paper. Transfer any remaining white and black nonpareils into separate small bowls.

3. Place the black and white decorating sugar and the jimmies in separate small shallow bowls. Tint the dark chocolate frosting black with the food coloring. Spoon 2 tablespoons of the vanilla frosting into a small ziplock bag and snip a ⅛-inch corner from the bag. Spread the tops of 5 of the cupcakes with the vanilla frosting and 4 with the chocolate frosting. Spread half the top of the remaining cupcake with vanilla frosting and the other half with black frosting. Roll the edges of some of the vanilla-frosted cupcakes in black sugar, jimmies, or nonpareils and some of the chocolate-frosted edges in the white (see page 12). For 2 of the cupcakes, use the black gel or the vanilla frosting to pipe several circles in a concentric pattern on top of a cupcake with the contrasting color of frosting. Use a round toothpick to lightly pull the gel and frosting in and out of the circles to create a design. For the remaining cupcakes, arrange the black and white candies and the chocolate cookies on top in your own designs.

PLAY POOL!

Cupcake form meets function in these cool-looking sugar-coated solids and stripes. The cue chalk, made from fruit chews, and perhaps a tablecloth cut from billiard-green felt complete the party scene. Hustlers young and old may find they prefer eating pool balls to pocketing them, so rack 'em up and clear the table.

If you can't find some of the colored decorating sugars, substitute white decorating sugar and tint it with food coloring. Rub the sugar with the food coloring in a ziplock bag to incorporate the color, then spread the sugar on a cookie sheet to dry before using.

15 vanilla cupcakes baked in green paper liners (see
   Sources, page 229)
1 vanilla cupcake baked in a white paper liner

2 cans (12 ounces each) whipped vanilla frosting
   Black food coloring (available at baking supply
   stores or see Sources)
1/4 cup each red, purple, dark green, yellow, orange,
   blue, dark red, and black decorating sugars (see
   headnote; available at baking supply stores or see
   Sources)
3/4 cup white decorating sugar (available at baking
   supply stores or see Sources)
15 white Necco Candy Wafers (or other white candy
   disks, such as candy melting wafers)
2 blue fruit chews (Starbursts)

1. Tint ¼ cup of the vanilla frosting black with the food coloring and spoon it into a ziplock bag. Press out the excess air, seal the bag, and set aside.

2. Cut fourteen 1-by-4-inch strips of wax paper. Place each of the colored decorating sugars in a small shallow bowl. Spread the tops of 7 of the cupcakes in the green paper liners with about half of the vanilla frosting, mounding it slightly. Place 2 wax paper strips, 1¼ inches apart, on either side of the cupcakes, leaving a band of exposed frosting in the center. Lightly press the strips into the frosting to remove any air pockets. Roll each of the cupcake tops in a different color sugar (not the black sugar) to coat the exposed frosting completely. Place the cupcakes in the freezer to set for 5 to 10 minutes.

3. Place the white decorating sugar in a small shallow bowl. Carefully peel the wax paper strips from the top of the chilled cupcakes and gently roll the exposed white frosting on either side of the colored band into the white sugar to coat completely, pressing the frosting against the sugar to smooth out any imperfections.

4. Spread the tops of the remaining 8 cupcakes in the green paper liners and the 1 cupcake in the white paper liner with the remaining vanilla frosting, mounding it slightly. Starting at the edge, roll each of the cupcakes in the green liners in a different color sugar, including black, to cover completely. Roll the top of the cupcake in the white liner in the white sugar to make the cue ball.

5. Snip a $1/16$-inch corner from the bag with the black frosting. Pipe the numbers from 1 to 15 onto the Necco wafers. Pipe a dot of black frosting on top of all the cupcakes except the cue ball and attach the Necco wafers to the appropriate colored balls.

6. Press the 2 blue fruit chews together to make a cube for the cue chalk. Press the end of a wooden spoon handle into one end of the cube to make the indentation for the cue.

BABY SHOWER

Cupcakes are the perfect bring-along for a baby shower. They're easy to pack in a box and just as easy to pass around. Each of these cutie-pies is made from two cupcakes, a mini sitting atop a standard.

15 standard vanilla cupcakes baked in pastel paper liners

15 mini vanilla cupcakes baked in white paper liners

8 pastel mini marshmallows

1/2 cup light blue (or pink or yellow) candy melting wafers (available at baking supply stores or see Sources, page 229)

2 cans (16 ounces each) vanilla frosting
Red food coloring

1/2 cup dark chocolate frosting

1 teaspoon instant coffee (brown food coloring also works but is flavorless)

1 tablespoon warm water

6 red fruit chews (Starbursts, Jolly Ranchers, Airheads)

1 cup white mini marshmallows

5 bear-shaped graham crackers, honey flavor (Teddy Grahams)

1 6-inch piece red fruit leather (Fruit by the Foot)

1 strand red licorice lace

5 red cereal O's (Fruit Loops)
Flower decors

SAFETY PINS
Makes 16 safety pins (1 extra in case of breakage)

1. Using clean scissors, cut the pastel mini marshmallows in half crosswise. With the sticky side down, trim one side of each marshmallow half with scissors to

create a semicircle for the head of the safety pin. Place the template for the safety pin (page 137) on a cookie sheet and cover with wax paper.

2. Place the blue candy melting wafers in a ziplock bag. Do not seal the bag. Microwave for 10 seconds to soften. Massage the wafers in the bag, return to the microwave, and repeat the process until the candy is smooth, about 30 seconds total (see page 16). Press out the excess air and seal the bag. Snip a $1/16$-inch corner from the bag. Pipe an outline of the safety pin on the wax paper. While the melted candy is still wet, add a trimmed marshmallow piece, curved side in, to the head of the safety pin as the clasp. Repeat the process until you have 16 safety pins. Refrigerate until set, about 5 minutes.

BABIES
Makes 15 babies

1. Spoon $3/4$ cup of the vanilla frosting into a ziplock bag. Tint 3 tablespoons of the vanilla frosting red with the food coloring and spoon it into a ziplock bag. Spoon the chocolate frosting into a ziplock bag. Press out the excess air in each of the bags, seal, and set aside. Dissolve the instant coffee in the warm water. Divide the remaining vanilla frosting into 3 separate bowls. Tint one part pale pink with a very small amount of red food coloring, one part pale beige with a few drops of the coffee, and one part tan with a few drops of the coffee and a touch of red food coloring. Cover the frostings with plastic wrap to prevent drying.

2. Snip a $1/8$-inch corner from the bag with the vanilla frosting. Cut 1 of the red fruit chews into 5 pieces. For the nipple on the baby bottle, roll each piece into a chocolate chip shape. Pipe a dot of white frosting on one of the flat ends of a white mini marshmallow and attach the nipple. Repeat with the remaining 4 fruit-chew pieces to make 5 baby bottles. Roll out the remaining 5 fruit chews on wax paper to $1/8$ inch thick and cut out bibs using the bib template as a guide. Using clean scissors, cut the remaining white mini marshmallows crosswise into thirds.

3. Spread the tops of 5 each of the standard cupcakes and 5 each of the mini cupcakes with the pink, beige, and tan frostings, mounding it slightly. Arrange 7 or 8 pieces of the cut mini marshmallows along the top edge of each of the mini cupcakes to make the bonnet.

4. Pipe a thin, wavy line of vanilla frosting around the edge of each of the standard cupcakes. Carefully peel the candy safety pins from the wax paper and press one pin into the wavy line of frosting at the edge of each standard cupcake.

5. Snip a $^1/_{16}$-inch corner from the bag with the chocolate frosting. Pipe eyelids and eyelashes on the mini cupcakes and a belly button, just above the safety pin, on each of the standard cupcakes. Pipe eyes on the teddy bear cookies.

6. Cut five $^3/_4$-inch-long ovals from the red fruit leather and add as the mouth on 5 of the mini cupcakes. Snip a $^1/_{16}$-inch corner from the bag with the red frosting and pipe a line around the edge of each oval. Pipe a red nose on the teddy bear cookies. Cut the red licorice lace into five $1^1/_2$-inch lengths. For each pacifier, press the licorice ends together and insert the ends into the hole in one of the red cereal O's. Press the pacifiers into the frosting on 5 of the mini cupcakes.

7. Matching like colors, place the mini cupcakes on their sides on top of the standard cupcakes, with the frosting facing the safety pin. For the bibbed babies, arrange the head slightly to one side, with the safety pin to the other side. Position the top of the bib at the baby's head. Pipe a few dots of vanilla frosting on the bib and add the flower decors. Add the teddy bear cookies to the open-mouthed babies, securing them with a dot of frosting. Add the bottles to the 5 babies without mouths, pressing the nipple into the frosting.

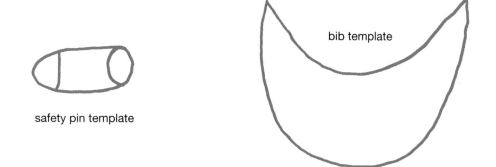

bib template

safety pin template

PETITS FOURS

The decorations on these petits fours are so pretty it will look like you flew to Paris and brought back dessert. The cupcakes are perfect for a baby or bridal shower, a Sweet Sixteen party, Easter, or an afternoon tea.

25 mini vanilla cupcakes baked in white paper liners

 1 can (16 ounces) vanilla frosting
    Red, yellow, purple, neon green, and blue food
    coloring (available at baking supply stores or see
    Sources, page 229)

1. Spoon $1/4$ cup of the vanilla frosting into a ziplock bag, press out the excess air, and seal. Divide the remaining vanilla frosting into 5 small microwavable bowls. Tint each bowl a different pastel color with the food coloring. Cover the frostings with plastic wrap until ready to use to prevent them from drying out.

2. Line a cookie sheet with wax paper. Working with one bowl of frosting at a time, heat in the microwave, stirring frequently, until it is the texture of lightly whipped cream, 4 to 5 seconds (see page 18).

3. Holding a cupcake by its paper liner, dip it into the frosting just up to the edge of the liner, 5 cupcakes of each color. After dipping, hold the cupcake above the surface and allow the excess frosting to drip back into the bowl. Carefully invert the cupcake and place on the cookie sheet. When the frosting becomes too thick, microwave for several seconds, stirring frequently.

4. Snip a $1/16$-inch corner from the bag with the vanilla frosting. Pipe small decorations on each cupcake, using the same decorations on each set of colors (keep the decorations minimal for a more sophisticated look).

5. Arrange the cupcakes on a serving platter in 5 rows of 5 cupcakes.

GARDEN PARTY

A garden plan should always include veggies the kids will eat, like candy-coated chocolate peas, taffy radishes, fruit-chew carrots, and frosted-flake lettuce. Our cupcake garden includes rows of freshly turned chocolate earth, chewy licorice vines, and a summer harvest of sweet vegetables sure to please a crowd.

24 vanilla cupcakes baked in white paper liners

 2 whole graham crackers

 2 sticks mint chewing gum

1/4 cup white chocolate melting wafers (available at baking supply stores or see Sources, page 229)

 6 thin pretzel sticks

 1 cup vanilla frosting
   Green, red, orange, and blue food coloring (available at baking supply stores or see Sources)

 1 can (16 ounces) chocolate frosting

 2 cups chocolate cookie crumbs (Oreos, Famous Chocolate Wafers)

 1 cup cornflakes

 9 green fruit chews (Jolly Ranchers)

 1 vanilla fruit chew (Tootsie Roll Midgee, Airhead)

 4 red fruit chews (Jolly Ranchers)

 8 orange fruit chews (Starbursts)

 1 teaspoon ground cinnamon

20 green candy-coated chocolates (M&M's)
   Green licorice laces (Kellogg's Watermelon Madness Fruit Streamers)

 2 teaspoons multicolored chocolate-covered sunflower seeds (available at gourmet candy stores or see Sources)

1. Using a serrated knife, cut the graham crackers in half crosswise. Cut each stick of gum into a $3/4$-inch-long triangle and pinch on one side to make the shovel blades. Line a cookie sheet with wax paper. Place the white chocolate melting wafers in a ziplock bag. Do not seal the bag. Microwave for 10 seconds to soften. Massage the chocolates in the bag, return to the microwave, and repeat the process until the chocolate is smooth, about 30 seconds total (see page 16). Press out the excess air and seal the bag.

2. Snip a $1/8$-inch corner from the bag and pipe an outline around each graham cracker. Fill in with more chocolate and spread into a smooth, thin layer to cover the cracker. Place on the cookie sheet and refrigerate until set, about 5 minutes.

3. Turn each cracker over and pipe a line of melted chocolate down the center of the uncoated side. Place a pretzel stick on top of the line of chocolate, leaving about a 2-inch overhang. Refrigerate until set. Cut the remaining 2 pretzel sticks into two 2-inch and two $3/4$-inch lengths. Pipe a small dot of melted chocolate on one end of the 2-inch pretzel stick and attach the smaller pretzel piece crosswise to make the shovel handle. Attach the gum shovel blade to the other end of the pretzel with a dot of melted chocolate. Place on the cookie sheet and refrigerate until set, about 5 minutes.

4. Tint $1/2$ cup of the vanilla frosting green with the food coloring. Tint 1 tablespoon of the vanilla frosting red. Tint 2 tablespoons of the vanilla frosting orange. Tint $1/4$ cup of the vanilla frosting blue. Spoon each color, including the remaining 1 tablespoon vanilla frosting, into separate ziplock bags, press out the excess air, and seal. Spoon $1/4$ cup of the chocolate frosting into a ziplock bag, press out the excess air, and seal. Snip a $1/16$-inch corner from each of the bags. Pipe the vegetable names in chocolate frosting and the vegetable shapes in the colored frostings on top of the chocolate-coated side of the graham crackers. Pipe a blue line of frosting around the border of each sign.

5. Place the chocolate cookie crumbs in a medium bowl. Spread the remaining chocolate frosting over the tops of the cupcakes. Starting at the edge, roll the tops of the cupcakes in the crumbs to cover completely. Arrange the cupcakes in 4 rows of 6 on a serving platter.

6. Work on one vegetable at a time.

LETTUCE
Makes 4 lettuce cupcakes

Line a cookie sheet with wax paper. Place the cornflakes in a small bowl. Spoon the remaining green frosting into a small microwavable bowl. Microwave the frosting, stirring frequently, until it is smooth and has the texture of lightly whipped cream, 5 to 10 seconds (see page 18). Pour the frosting over the cornflakes, toss well to coat, and spread the cornflakes onto the cookie sheet. Refrigerate until set, about 10 minutes. Cut 2 of the green fruit chews in half and shape into balls. Place 1 green ball on top of each of 4 cupcakes and arrange 8 to 12 green-frosted cornflakes around the balls to make the leaves. Secure with a dot of green frosting, if necessary.

RADISHES
Makes 4 radish cupcakes

For each radish, cut the vanilla fruit chew into quarters. Roll 1 red fruit chew together with 1 vanilla piece, keeping the colors separate, and shape into a ball. Pinch the white end to form the radish root. Place 1 radish on top of each of 4 cupcakes, and add several green-frosted cornflakes for the leaves.

CARROTS
Makes 5 carrot cupcakes

Cut 2 of the orange fruit chews in half and shape each piece into a small carrot. Shape the remaining 6 fruit chews into 6 large carrots. Score the side of each carrot with a knife. Rub the sides of the carrots with the cinnamon to make them look freshly pulled from the garden. Use a round toothpick to make a small hole in the large end of each carrot. Cut 2 of the green fruit chews into thin strips and roll each strip between your fingers to look like carrot tops. Press 4 or 5 strips into the hole in the top of each carrot. Arrange the carrots, overlapping slightly, on top of 5 cupcakes.

PEAS
Makes 5 pea-pod cupcakes

Roll out each of the remaining 5 green fruit chews into a 3-by-1-inch oval $\frac{1}{8}$ inch thick. Press 4 green candy-coated chocolates onto one side of each oval. Fold the other side over to cover the candies slightly. Pinch the ends and place 1 pea pod on top of each of 5 cupcakes. Cut the green licorice laces into various lengths and arrange them around the pea pods to make the vines.

SHOVELS AND SIGNS
Makes 4 seed-pack cupcakes and 2 shovel cupcakes

Insert the pretzel end of each seed-pack sign into the top of each of 4 cupcakes and place at the head of the rows. Insert the shovel blades into the frosting on top of 2 cupcakes, scatter a few sunflower seeds around the shovels, and place in the rows with the radishes and lettuce.

EASTER EGGS

These eggs just may upstage the bunny. The egg-shaped graham crackers are coated with frosting and decorated with sparkling sugars and a rainbow assortment of candies. For half of the cupcakes, the sugar coating goes on first, and for the other half, the candies are applied before the sugar, creating a subtle difference in the brightly colored tones. Just think: when you make these Easter eggs, you can eat cupcakes all week long instead of egg salad sandwiches. How great is that?

12 chocolate cupcakes baked in white paper liners

1 can (16 ounces) plus 1 cup vanilla frosting
  Green, yellow, orange, purple, and pink food coloring (available at baking supply stores or see Sources, page 229)

12 honey graham crackers

1/2 cup each blue, violet, pink, and yellow decorating sugars (available at baking supply stores or see Sources)

2 tablespoons each mini and regular flower candy decors, mini and regular dot decors, and stick decors (available at baking supply stores or see Sources)

1. Tint 1 1/2 cups of the vanilla frosting light green. Spoon 1 cup of green frosting into a ziplock bag. Reserve the remaining 1/2 cup. Tint 2 tablespoons each of the vanilla frosting yellow, orange, light purple, and pink, and spoon into separate small ziplock bags. Spoon 2 tablespoons of the vanilla frosting into a small ziplock bag. Press out the excess air in each of the bags, seal, and set aside.

2. Using a serrated knife, trim each graham cracker to fit the template shape. Put a small dollop of the green frosting on top of the cupcakes and place 1 graham-cracker egg on each cupcake, pressing down to secure. The crackers will extend over the edge of the cupcakes.

3. Place each color of decorating sugar on a small shallow plate, such as a saucer. Spoon the remaining vanilla frosting into a ziplock bag, press out the excess air, and seal. Snip a $\frac{1}{2}$-inch corner from the bag. Working on one cracker at a time, spread frosting on top of the cracker and spread it in a smooth, even layer to cover the top. For 6 of the cupcakes, arrange the decors in a pattern on top of the frosting, using tweezers, then carefully roll the top of the cracker in the desired color of sugar to cover completely. For the remaining 6 cupcakes, roll the frosted crackers in the desired color of sugar first, then arrange the decors in a pattern on top of the crackers.

4. Snip a $\frac{1}{16}$-inch corner from the small bags with the yellow, orange, purple, pink, and vanilla frosting. Pipe dots, lines, and dashes of frosting on top of the sugar-coated crackers. Snip a $\frac{1}{8}$-inch corner from the bag with the green frosting and pipe pulled dots of frosting around the base of each egg, covering the top of the cupcake.

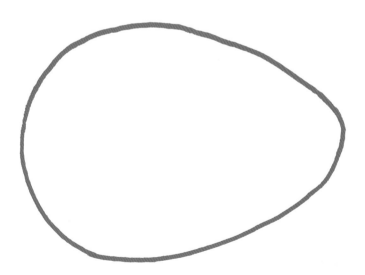

RABBIT HOLES

There's a good reason you've never seen the Easter Rabbit: quick as a bunny, he jumps back into his hole to hide. This cupcaking project focuses on the business end of the bunny. His tail is a mini marshmallow coated in nonpareils, his feet are white circus peanuts, the grass is frosting, and the hole he's disappearing into is a coating of dark chocolate cookie crumbs.

24 vanilla cupcakes baked in green paper liners (see
   Sources, page 229)

1 cup chocolate frosting
$^1/_2$ cup chocolate cookie crumbs (Oreos, Famous
   Chocolate Wafers)
1 can (16 ounces) plus 1 cup vanilla frosting
   Green and yellow food coloring
   Assorted malted milk eggs and jelly beans
2 tablespoons flower candy decors (Cake Mate)
8 white circus peanuts
4 small black jelly beans
24 brown chocolate-covered sunflower seeds (available
   at gourmet candy stores or see Sources)
4 mini marshmallows
1 teaspoon light corn syrup
1 tablespoon white nonpareils (available at baking
   supply stores or see Sources)

1. Spoon 2 tablespoons of the chocolate frosting into a small ziplock bag, press out the excess air, and seal. Place the chocolate cookie crumbs in a small shallow bowl. Spread the remaining chocolate frosting on top of 4 of the cupcakes. Starting on the edge, roll the tops in the cookie crumbs to cover completely.

2. Arrange all the cupcakes on a serving platter in 4 rows of 6, distributing the chocolate-crumbed cupcakes randomly throughout.

3. Tint 1 cup of the vanilla frosting light green with the green and yellow food coloring. Tint the remaining vanilla frosting bright green. Spoon some of the light green frosting into one side of a ziplock bag and spoon some of the darker green frosting into the other side of the bag. Press out the excess air and seal the bag. Snip a 1/8-inch corner from the bag. Using a squeeze-and-pull motion, pipe grass on top of the remaining cupcakes. Pipe along the edge of the cupcake first, then work in concentric circles toward the center, each row slightly overlapping the previous row (see the fur technique on page 15).

4. Arrange the malted milk eggs and jelly beans in clusters on the cupcakes. Sprinkle the tops of the cupcakes with the flower decors.

5. For the feet, cut the circus peanuts in half lengthwise (only the flat bottom portion will be used). Cut the black jelly beans in half lengthwise. Snip a 1/8-inch corner from the bag with the chocolate frosting. For each foot, pipe 4 small dots of frosting on the smooth flat side of the peanut. Add a jelly bean half, lengthwise, and 3 brown sunflower seeds to make the pads of the foot. Press 2 feet onto each of the chocolate cupcakes, spacing them slightly apart and allowing them to extend over the edge of the cupcake. Roll the mini marshmallows in the corn syrup and then in the white nonpareils to make the tails. Press the tail onto the cupcake just above the feet.

CANDY STARS AND STRIPES FOREVER

Oh, say, can you see all the candy on these cupcakes? Everyone will find a favorite cupcake here, because each one has its own unique decoration. With 48 mini cupcakes and 48 standard cupcakes, this project will feed your extended family or the whole neighborhood. Got fewer patriots in your gathering? Make the Red on Red variation.

48 standard vanilla cupcakes baked in white paper liners
6 mini vanilla cupcakes baked in white paper liners
42 mini vanilla cupcakes baked in red paper liners (see Sources, page 229)

3 cans (16 ounces each) vanilla frosting
Blue and red food coloring
Assorted red and white candies:
   Swedish Fish, regular and mini
   Fruit leather (Fruit by the Foot)
   Candy-coated chocolates, regular and mini
      (M&M's)
   Jordan Almonds
   Gumdrops and spice drops
   Sprinkles and jimmies
   Gumballs and gum rectangles (Chiclets)
   Jelly beans
   Licorice Pastels, licorice laces, nibs, and twists
   Gummy bears
   Mini jawbreakers
   Sour strips and fruit chews (Sour Power Belts,
      Sour Patch Kids)

1. Tint 1¾ cups of the vanilla frosting blue with the food coloring. Tint 2 cups of the vanilla frosting red with the food coloring.

2. Spread the blue frosting on the tops of 12 of the standard cupcakes and the 6 mini cupcakes in white liners and smooth. Arrange the white candies on top in decorative designs.

3. Spread the red frosting on the tops of the 42 mini cupcakes in red liners and smooth. Arrange the red candies on top in decorative designs. Spread the remaining 36 standard cupcakes with the remaining vanilla frosting and smooth.

4. Starting at the bottom of the flag, arrange 3 rows across of 8 white-frosted cupcakes on a large serving platter or cutting board. Arrange the top 3 rows with 4 blue-frosted (on the left) and 4 white-frosted cupcakes. Make sure all the cupcakes are touching one another. Place the mini red cupcakes between the rows of white-frosted cupcakes; 2 rows of 12 bridging the bottom 3 rows and 3 rows of 6 bridging the top 3 rows. Place the 6 mini blue cupcakes in between the rows of blue-frosted cupcakes.

VARIATION

Red on Red
Follow the directions for the red mini cupcakes and serve them as a solid color on a white platter or cutting board.

Our Family

FAMILY TREE

Turn those funny family quirks into quirky family cupcakes. Start with a photo of each family member and examine it for special traits (be kind: you don't want to start a feud). Unique hair and creative accessories can help mimic your family members. Grandma's bouffant hairdo, dad's beer bottle, or cousin Sally's hockey stick all add humorous touches while helping to identify the cupcake likenesses. You can make a tree for your project by cutting colored paper for branches and leaves. (Karen's mother-in-law, Barbara, painted ours.)

To get started, make a quick sketch of each family member on a piece of paper. Choose from the eyes, mouths, and hairstyles shown on pages 2 and 3 or go crazy and create your own. Make any templates you need for hair or accessories and, using the melted-candy drawing technique (see page 16), pipe the designs on wax paper, then place them in the refrigerator to harden. Organize the candy for the eyes, nose, mouth, ears, and hair. Try to keep things simple; use one or two kinds of candy for all the eyes, ears, and noses, turning or trimming them where possible to vary the shapes. Frost the cupcakes in an appropriate color, add the hair, facial expressions, and accessories, and place on the tree design in a position that reflects the family connections.

WEDDING CAKE
AND MONOGRAMS

Wait till they serve this cake to bite your husband's head off. Here's a simple way to create a sophisticated wedding cake. Sugar-dusted white chocolate flowers accented with silver dragées and silver-dusted white chocolate leaves give the cake a lush, romantic feeling. The elegant bride and groom are made of chocolate, with vanilla-wafer faces.

We recommend using one of our homemade cake recipes (pages 220–225) and topping the cupcakes with a dreamy buttercream frosting (page 227). A tiered platter gives the cupcake layers a perfect "wedding cake" profile. The four-tiered design uses 30 cupcakes, but you can make extra wedding band-, flower-, and leaf-topped cupcakes to feed a crowd. And you can personalize additional cupcakes for the bridal party with sophisticated monograms (see page 161).

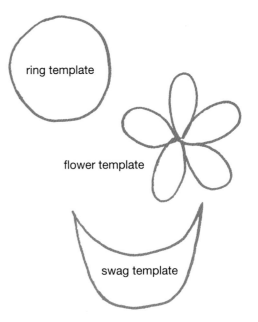

ring template

flower template

swag template

1 jumbo vanilla cupcake baked in a silver foil liner
30 standard vanilla cupcakes baked in silver foil liners

1 large bunch lemon leaves (or substitute mint leaves and make twice as many)
3 cups white chocolate melting wafers (available at baking supply stores or see Sources, page 229)
2 mini vanilla wafers (Nabisco Mini Nilla Wafers)
1/2 cup white decorating sugar (available at baking supply stores or see Sources)
1/2 cup dark cocoa melting wafers (available at baking supply stores or see Sources)

1 container (2 g) Nu Silver luster dust
   (see Sources)
3 tablespoons chocolate frosting
3½ cups vanilla frosting
   White flower candy decors (Cake
   Mate)
   White pearl dragées (see Sources)
3 tablespoons silver dragées (see
   Sources)
2 teaspoons lemon extract
1 cup white coarse decorating sugar
   (available at baking supply stores or
   see Sources)
½ cup mini silver dragées (see Sources)
   4-tiered cake stand (available at home
   decorating stores or see Sources)

bride and groom
templates

1. Remove the lemon leaves from the branches. Wash the leaves with warm water and pat dry on paper towels. Arrange the bride and groom, ring, flower, and swag templates (page 156) on 2 cookie sheets and line with wax paper. Line 2 more cookie sheets with wax paper. Place 1 cup of the white chocolate melting wafers in a ziplock bag. Do not seal the bag. Microwave for 10 seconds to soften. Massage the chocolates in the bag, return to the microwave, and repeat the process until the chocolate is smooth, about 1 minute total (see page 16). Press out the excess air and seal the bag.

2. Snip a ⅛-inch corner from the bag. Pipe an outline of the bride with the melted chocolate and fill in with more chocolate, making 1 bride. Tap the pan slightly to flatten. While the chocolate is still wet, push 1 mini vanilla wafer, flat side down, into the chocolate for the head. Pipe outlines for 10 rings, 8 swags, and 41 flowers. While the chocolate is still wet, sprinkle the tops of the flowers with the white decorating sugar. Refrigerate until set, about 5 minutes.

3. Place the dark cocoa melting wafers in a ziplock bag. Do not seal the bag. Microwave for 10 seconds to soften. Massage the chocolate in the bag, return to the microwave, and repeat the process until the chocolate is smooth, about 35 seconds total. Press out the excess air and seal the bag.

4. Snip a ⅛-inch corner from the bag. Pipe an outline of the groom-and-hat template with the melted chocolate and fill in with more chocolate, making 1 groom. Tap the pan slightly to flatten. While the chocolate is still wet, push 1 mini vanilla wafer, flat side down, into the chocolate for the head. Pipe the brim of the hat, overlapping the vanilla wafer slightly. Refrigerate until set, about 5 minutes.

5. Place 1 cup of the remaining white chocolate melting wafers in a microwavable bowl and microwave, stirring occasionally, until the chocolate is smooth, about 1 minute. Using a small, clean craft brush or your fingertip, coat the top side of each lemon leaf with an even layer of chocolate. Place the leaves on the prepared cookie sheets. Add more white chocolate melting wafers as necessary and microwave, stirring occasionally, until smooth. You'll need about 50 leaves. Place the cookie sheets in the refrigerator until the chocolate is set, about 5 minutes.

6. When the chocolate has hardened, carefully peel away the lemon leaf; it will come off surprisingly easily. Use a toothpick or clean tweezers to remove any small pieces of leaf that may remain (the leaves and other chocolate decorations can be made up to 5 days in advance and kept in a cool, dry place). Before placing the chocolate leaves on the cake, brush the textured side with the luster dust.

7. Spoon the chocolate frosting and ½ cup of the vanilla frosting into separate ziplock bags, press out the excess air, and seal. Snip a ¹⁄₁₆-inch corner from each bag. Using the chocolate frosting, pipe hair on the vanilla wafers for the bride and the groom. Using tweezers, place flower decors in the bride's hair. Using the vanilla frosting, pipe lines on the bride's dress to make gathers and folds. Pipe dots of frosting at the hem, neckline, and waist, then use tweezers to place pearl dragées at the hem and neck and flower decors and pearl dragées at the waist. For the groom's shirt, start on either side of the neck and pipe a V-shaped outline of vanilla frosting extending down about 1 inch, then fill in. Pipe a white hatband, 3 dots for buttons, and 1 dot on the lapel. Use tweezers to place pearl dragées in the button positions and a flower decor on the lapel. Pipe a dot of vanilla frosting in the center of each of the 41 white chocolate flowers and add a silver dragée. Dissolve about ½ teaspoon luster dust in the lemon extract and brush the tops of the 10 white chocolate rings with the mixture.

8. Place the white coarse decorating sugar and the mini silver dragées in separate small bowls. Spread the tops of the cupcakes with the remaining vanilla frosting. Edge 5 of the cupcakes in the mini silver dragées (see page 12). Starting on the edge, roll the jumbo cupcake in the coarse sugar to cover completely. Edge 17 of the cupcakes in the remaining coarse sugar (see page 12). Arrange 5 of the white chocolate flowers on the remaining 8 cupcakes, positioning 4 of them along the edge, at the points of the compass, and 1 on top. Press about 4 silver dragées along the edge in between the flowers. Place the rings, 2 per cupcake, on top of the 5 cupcakes edged with the mini silver dragées. Arrange 1 or 2 chocolate leaves on top of each of the 17 cupcakes edged in coarse sugar. Carefully insert the bride and groom in the top of the jumbo cupcake. Carefully arrange the swag pieces of white chocolate around the edge of the jumbo cupcake. Pipe dots of vanilla frosting along the edge where the swags join and attach a silver dragée.

9. Arrange the cupcakes on a tiered serving platter: leaf cupcakes on the bottom, followed by the flowered cupcakes, the ring cupcakes, and the jumbo cupcake with the bride and groom. Arrange the extra chocolate leaves around the cupcakes.

MONOGRAM VARIATION

A monogram is the very best way to say, "This is mine!"
Serve these personalized cupcakes at weddings, showers, birthdays, family gatherings, school events, or even a business event. Roll out spice drops, gumdrops, fruit slices, or fruit leather. Use clean scissors or a small cookie cutter or knife to cut out desired letters. Or use small candies like chocolate-covered sunflower seeds, mini M&M's, Licorice Pastels, colored rock candy crystals, and candy decors and place them side by side with tweezers.

To make letters of frosting, make a practice sheet of letters and place a piece of wax paper on top. Practice on the wax paper until you feel comfortable. You can scrape off the frosting and use it again. Or use a round toothpick to score the letters on top of the cupcake first, then pipe over them.

CHOCOLATE DRAWING

Create your own lettering, make multiple templates, and place on a cookie sheet. Place a piece of wax paper on top of the template. Place any color candy melting wafers in a ziplock bag. Do not seal the bag. Microwave for 10 seconds to soften. Massage the wafers in the bag, return to the microwave, and repeat the process until the candy is smooth, about 30 seconds total (see page 16). Press out the excess air and seal the bag. Snip a $1/8$-inch corner from the bag. Pipe an outline of the letter on the wax paper and fill in. Tap the pan lightly after each letter to flatten. Refrigerate until set, about 5 minutes. Brush the top of the letters with some luster dust for added shine. For an even brighter shine, mix 1 teaspoon lemon extract with $1/4$ teaspoon luster dust, then brush on top of the chocolate letters. (Don't remove the letters from the wax paper before brushing.)

CHOCOLATE DRAWING WITH NONPAREILS

Follow the same method as for the chocolate drawing, but before the chocolate sets, sprinkle the top with the desired nonpareils. Continue as directed. (These may be made up to 1 week in advance and stored in an airtight container in a cool, dry place.)

Nightmare Before Thanksgiving

Halloween is the creepiest holiday of the year and the best time to make scary cupcakes. These bugs, aliens, bats, and wolves are perfect for trick or treat, school parties, or just a little late-night full-moon snacking.

ALIEN INVASION

A close encounter of the cupcake kind. The design is eerie yet simple. The aliens are made from marshmallows and doughnut holes attached to standard-sized cupcakes. They are dipped in store-bought icing that's been colored bilious green and zapped in the microwave to liquefy it for dipping. Each creepy little alien sits in its own space capsule made from plastic take-out containers, allowing for easy transport to a party in the next galaxy.

24 vanilla cupcakes baked in silver foil liners

2 cans (16 ounces each) vanilla frosting
   Neon green food coloring (McCormick)

12 marshmallows

24 plain doughnut holes

48 black chocolate-covered sunflower seeds (available
   at gourmet candy stores or see Sources, page 229)
   Black licorice laces, cut into 1-inch pieces

24 plastic take-out containers (available at baking or
   party supply stores or see Sources)

1. Tint the vanilla frosting green with the food coloring. Using clean scissors, cut the marshmallows in half crosswise.

2. Spread a thin layer of the green frosting on top of the cupcakes and place 1 marshmallow half in the center of each cupcake, cut side down. Add a dot of frosting to the marshmallow and place a doughnut hole on top of the marshmallow, pressing it into the frosting. Spread frosting over the marshmallow and the doughnut hole to fill in the gaps and smooth (see page 18).

3. Place the assembled cupcakes on a cookie sheet in the freezer for 10 to 15 minutes, or until slightly frozen.

4. Working in batches, spoon ¾ cup of the remaining frosting into a 1-cup glass measuring cup. Microwave for 10- to 15-second intervals, stirring frequently, until the frosting is the consistency of lightly whipped cream.

5. Holding a chilled cupcake by its foil liner, dip it into the frosting right up to the edge of the liner. Hold the cupcake above the surface and allow the excess frosting to drip off (see page 19). Carefully turn the cupcake right side up and place on a cookie sheet. Repeat with the remaining cupcakes. When the frosting becomes too thick, reheat in the microwave for several seconds, stirring well. Add more frosting and reheat as necessary.

6. Press the black sunflower seeds onto the head area, pointed ends in, to make the eyes. Using a round toothpick, make 2 holes in the top of each alien and insert a piece of licorice in each hole for the antennae.

7. Carefully place each cupcake into a plastic container and top with the lid.

CREEPY CRAWLERS

In the mood to swallow a scorpion, bite a tick, or chew a centipede? Then this confectionery entomology is for you. The candy-coated chocolates and nuts used for the head, thorax, and abdomen of the creepy crawlers are glued together with chocolate (see page 16). A specimen box purchased at a home-organization store is a cool idea for showcasing the cupcakes at a meeting of your local geek squad.

12 chocolate cupcakes baked in brown paper liners (see
    Sources, page 229)

Assortment of mini, regular, peanut, and mega
    candy-coated chocolates (a variety of M&M's)
Orange and brown chocolate-covered sunflower
    seeds (available at gourmet candy stores or see
    Sources)
1 cup dark cocoa melting wafers (available at baking
    supply stores or see Sources)
$^1/_2$ cup peanut butter chips (Reese's)
$^1/_2$ cup white coarse decorating sugar (available at
    baking supply stores or see Sources)
1 can (12 ounces) whipped vanilla frosting

1. Separate the candies by color for each insect: yellow Mega M&M's and brown chocolate-covered sunflower seeds for the spider; green M&M's Minis and M&M's Peanuts for the beetle; red M&M's for the centipede; tan and blue Mega M&M's and brown chocolate-covered sunflower seeds for the ticks; red Mega M&M's and M&M's Peanuts for the ant; and orange regular M&M's, M&M's Peanuts, chocolate-covered sunflower seeds, and peanut butter chips for the scorpion.

2. Place the 6 bug templates (page 170) on cookie sheets and cover with wax paper. Place the dark cocoa melting wafers in a ziplock bag. Do not seal the bag. Microwave for 10 seconds to soften. Massage the chocolate in the bag, return to the microwave, and repeat the process until the chocolate is smooth, about 1 minute total (see page 16). Press out the excess air and seal the bag.

3. Working on one bug template at a time (do not make the scorpion yet), snip a 1/16-inch corner from the bag and pipe the legs and antennae on the wax paper. Pipe the body, making sure you connect all the chocolate parts. While the chocolate is still wet, add the candies. Continue with the remaining chocolate and candies, making 2 ants, 2 spiders, 6 ticks, 2 centipedes, and 2 beetles. Refrigerate until set, about 5 minutes. Place the peanut butter chips in a ziplock bag. Do not seal the bag. Microwave for 10 seconds to soften. Massage the chips in the bag, return to the microwave, and repeat the process until the mixture is smooth, about 25 seconds total. Press out the excess air and seal the bag.

4. For the scorpion, snip a 1/16-inch corner from the bag and pipe the legs on the wax paper. Pipe the body and tail, making sure you connect all the parts. While the peanut butter mixture is still wet, add the orange candies. Make 2 scorpions. Refrigerate until set, about 5 minutes.

5. Place the white decorating sugar in a small shallow bowl. Spread the vanilla frosting on top of the cupcakes and smooth (see page 10). Roll the edges of the cupcakes in the sugar (see page 12).

6. Carefully peel the hardened insects from the wax paper and transfer to the cupcakes, pressing down slightly into the frosting to secure. For the tick, place 3 ticks on each cupcake.

BUG TEMPLATES

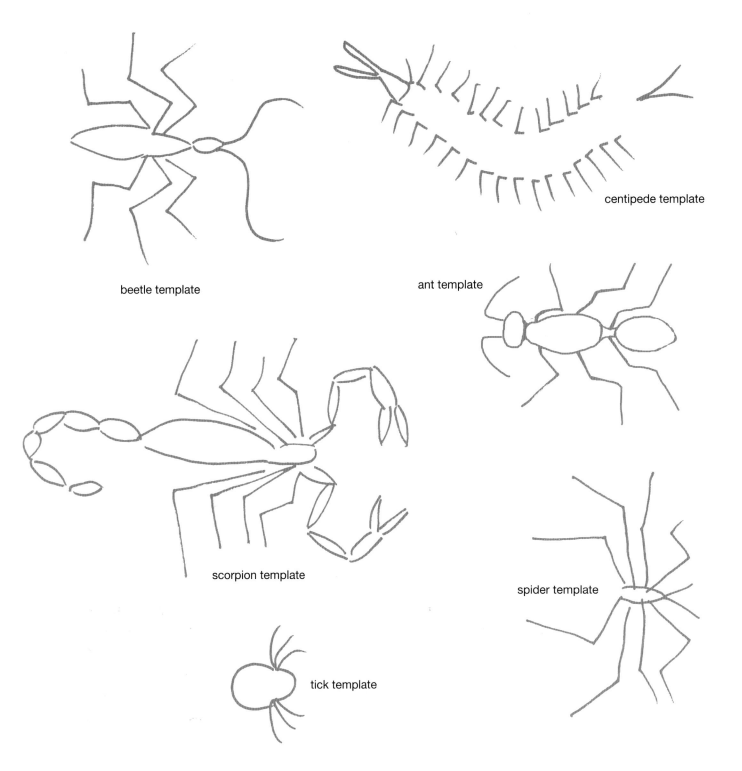

beetle template

centipede template

ant template

scorpion template

spider template

tick template

WHAT A HOOT!

Mama owl needs some really big eyes to watch out for her baby hooters, and making those big brown beauties is as easy as pulling apart an Oreo cookie. The pupils of Mama's eyes are Junior Mints and the babies' are M&M's. The beaks are yellow Runts and chocolate-covered sunflower seeds.

12 standard chocolate cupcakes baked in brown paper liners (see Sources, page 229)
24 mini chocolate cupcakes baked in brown paper liners (see Sources)

24 chocolate cream-filled sandwich cookies (Oreos)
48 mini chocolate cream-filled sandwich cookies (Mini Oreos)
 2 tablespoons vanilla frosting
 2 cans (16 ounces each) chocolate frosting
12 banana-shaped hard candies (Runts)
24 yellow chocolate-covered sunflower seeds (available at gourmet candy stores or see Sources)
24 mini chocolate-covered mints (Junior Mints)
48 brown mini candy-coated chocolates (M&M's Minis)

1. Microwave a few regular and mini cream-filled sandwich cookies at a time for several seconds (this will help keep the cream filling on one half when you separate the cookies). Be careful not to microwave the cookies for too long, or the filling will melt. Immediately twist each sandwich cookie apart so that you have a cream-covered side and a plain cookie side. Use a paring knife to remove any excess crumbs from the cream filling. Continue until all the cookies have been separated.

2. Using a serrated knife, make 2 parallel cuts ½ inch in from the edge on each regular plain cookie half (see page 20). The 2 outside pieces with the rounded edges will be used for the ears on the mama owls. Cut the mini plain cookie halves in half.

3. Spoon the vanilla frosting and 1½ cups of the chocolate frosting into separate ziplock bags, press out the excess air, seal, and set aside. Spread the remaining chocolate frosting on top of the cupcakes and smooth.

4. Using a little chocolate frosting, attach 2 of the large ear pieces, rounded sides in and about 1½ inches apart, on top of each of the 12 standard cupcakes. Angle the ears slightly away from each other and allow them to extend about ¾ inch beyond the edge of the cupcake. Repeat the process with the mini cookies and the mini cupcakes, placing the ears about ½ inch apart and allowing a ½-inch overhang.

5. Place 2 regular cream-sided cookie halves, cream side up, on the upper half of each standard cupcake to make the eyes. Do the same with the mini cream-sided cookie halves and the mini cupcakes.

6. Snip a ⅛-inch corner from the bags with the chocolate and vanilla frosting. Pipe lines of chocolate frosting along the length of the cookie ears to cover. Starting with the edge at the top of the cupcake, pipe the feathers with the chocolate frosting using the squeeze-and-pull fur technique (see page 15). Work inward from the edge in slightly overlapping rows until the section above the eyes is covered. On the standard cupcakes, pipe a few feathers on the edge just below each eye. On the mini cupcakes, pipe several small feathers along the edge beside each eye.

7. Press a yellow candy in the middle of each cupcake to make the beak: the banana-shaped candies on the standard cupcakes, the sunflower seeds on the mini cupcakes. Use a dot of vanilla frosting on the cream of each cookie to attach a chocolate-covered mint to the eyes on the standard cupcakes and a brown chocolate candy to the eyes on the mini cupcakes. Place the eyes in different positions to give the owls character. Using the vanilla frosting, pipe a white highlight on each eye.

PUMPKIN PATCH

One trip to the cupcake pumpkin patch, and this project will become a favorite fall tradition. It's a terrific dessert centerpiece for any gathering from Halloween to Thanksgiving. The pumpkin patch boasts both standard and mini cupcakes, and each one is a little different—just like a real pumpkin patch—so you can pick and choose your favorite.

12 standard Pumpkin Spice cupcakes (page 219) baked in orange paper liners (see Sources, page 229)

24 mini Pumpkin Spice cupcakes (page 219) baked in white paper liners

4 green licorice twists (Twizzlers Rainbow Twists)

1 can (16 ounces) plus 1 cup vanilla frosting
Orange food coloring (available at baking supply stores or see Sources)

1 cup orange decorating sugar (available at baking supply stores or see Sources)
Green licorice laces (Watermelon Madness Fruit Streamers)

1. Cut the licorice twists into thirty-six ³/₄-inch pieces for the pumpkin stems. Tint the vanilla frosting orange with the food coloring. Tint ¹/₂ cup of the orange frosting a darker shade of orange with more food coloring, and spoon into a ziplock bag. Press out the excess air, seal the bag, and set aside.

2. Place the orange decorating sugar in a shallow bowl. Spread the lighter orange frosting on top of the cupcakes, mounding it slightly (see page 11). Starting on the edge, roll the cupcake tops in the sugar to cover completely.

3. Use a wooden skewer to mark ridges in the top of each cupcake. Starting in the center or slightly off center, lightly press the skewer down toward the top of the paper liner to create 5 or 6 indentations. Snip a ¹/₁₆-inch corner from the bag

with the darker orange frosting and pipe a line in each indentation to make the ribs. Insert a cut green twist for the stem. Arrange the cupcakes on a serving platter or a cutting board and add the green licorice laces, trimmed to various lengths, for the tendrils.

HOWLING WEREWOLVES

This pack of cupcakes will scare up a howling good time. Their fiery red fruit-leather mouths and neon candy eyes will send a chill down your spine. The snouts, cut from marshmallows, are shaped to bark, yelp, yap, and bay at the moon.

12 vanilla cupcakes baked in yellow paper liners

12 chocolate cupcakes baked in brown paper liners (see Sources, page 229)

MOON AND BAT
Makes 12 cupcakes

¹/₄ cup each yellow and white decorating sugars (available at baking supply stores or see Sources)

1 can (12 ounces) whipped vanilla frosting

12 thin chocolate cookies (Famous Chocolate Wafers)

12 brown candy-coated chocolates (M&M's)

1. Combine the yellow and white sugars together in a small shallow bowl. Spread the vanilla frosting on top of the 12 vanilla cupcakes, mounding it in the center (see page 11). Starting at the edge, roll the tops of the cupcakes in the sugars to cover completely.

2. Heat the chocolate cookies in the microwave for 5 seconds to soften. Using a serrated knife, cut the chocolate cookies in half. With a small paring knife, cut a scalloped edge along the straight side of each cookie half to make the wings (see page 20). Insert 2 wings, side by side, into the frosting on top of each cupcake. Add a brown chocolate candy between the wings to make the body of the bat.

Makes 12 cupcakes

1/2 cup vanilla frosting

1 cup dark chocolate frosting

Black food coloring (available at baking supply stores or see Sources, page 229)

1 can (16 ounces) chocolate frosting

24 marshmallows

Red fruit leather (Fruit by the Foot)

8 each orange, yellow, and green candy-coated chocolates (M&M's)

12 black jelly beans

1. Spoon the vanilla frosting into a ziplock bag, press out the excess air, and seal. Tint the dark chocolate frosting black with the food coloring. Spoon half of the black frosting up one side of a ziplock bag. Spoon half of the chocolate frosting up the other side of the bag. Press out the excess air and seal the bag. Repeat the process with the remaining frosting in another ziplock bag. Press out the excess air and seal the bag.

2. To make the ears, lay 12 of the marshmallows on their sides and cut off both of the corners at one end, angling your knife so that the cut side will be about 1 inch wide. Use the remaining 12 marshmallows to make the muzzles by cutting a 1/2- to 1-inch V-shaped notch from the end of each marshmallow (see photo, opposite page). The size of the notch will determine the size of the mouth.

3. Snip a 1/8-inch corner from one of the bags with the chocolate frosting. Pipe a small dot of frosting on the cut side of each ear and on the flat side of the muzzle. Attach the ears on either side at the top of each chocolate cupcake and place the muzzle just below the center. Cut 1- or 2-inch-long ovals from the red fruit leather to fit the notched mouth openings and press into the notches of the muzzles to stick. Trim off any excess fruit leather with clean scissors.

4. Working on one cupcake at a time, pipe several lines of chocolate frosting along the length of the ears to cover. Starting at the edge, pipe a 1/2-inch border around the cupcake using the fur technique (see page 15), always pulling the frosting away from the center. Pipe another row inside the first, slightly overlapping the rows. Continue piping concentric rows of frosting, covering the

cupcake and working your way up the marshmallow snout to the open mouth. Repeat with the remaining cupcakes and the second bag of chocolate frosting.

5. Press 2 chocolate candies of a matching color, edges in and at an angle, into the frosting to make the glowing eyes. Snip a ¹/₈-inch corner from the bag with the vanilla frosting and pipe sharp fangs all around the edge of the fruit leather, using a squeeze-and-pull motion. Add a black jelly bean, crosswise, for the nose.

AUTUMN LEAVES

For fall gatherings—everything from back-to-school to Thanksgiving—this colorful wreath makes an elegant centerpiece. The leaves are created by painting melted candy wafers on maple leaves, letting it harden, then peeling off the leaf to reveal a stunning edible replica.

24 chocolate cupcakes baked in brown paper liners (see Sources, page 229)

100 small fresh maple leaves

1 cup orange candy melting wafers (available at baking supply stores or see Sources)

1 cup green candy melting wafers (available at baking supply stores or see Sources)

1 cup milk chocolate melting wafers (available at baking supply stores or see Sources)

1 bag (14 ounces) caramels, unwrapped

3/4 cup chocolate jimmies

1 can (16 ounces) chocolate frosting

1. Wash the maple leaves with warm water and pat dry on paper towels. Line several cookie sheets with wax paper. Place the orange candy, green candy, and milk chocolate melting wafers into separate microwavable bowls. Microwave each bowl separately, stirring occasionally, until the candy is smooth, about 1 minute. Using a small, clean craft brush or your fingertip, paint spots in the 3 different colors of melted candy in an even layer (not too thin) over the top side of each leaf (see page 159). While the candy is still wet, swirl the colors slightly to blend. Place the leaf on one of the cookie sheets, coated side up. Repeat with the remaining leaves. If the candy becomes too thick, reheat in the microwave for several seconds, stirring frequently. Place the cookie sheets in the refrigerator until the candy is set, about 5 minutes.

2. Carefully peel the leaves from the hardened candy. They come off surprisingly easily. Use a toothpick or clean tweezers to remove any small pieces of leaf that may remain. (The leaves and other candy pieces can be made up to 5 days in advance, covered, and kept in a cool dry place.)

3. Line a cookie sheet with wax paper. Spoon the remaining milk chocolate into a small bowl to use for the acorn tops. Soften 4 or 5 caramels at a time in the microwave for 3 to 4 seconds. Roll each caramel into an acorn (egg) shape. Place the chocolate jimmies in a small shallow bowl. Reheat the milk chocolate in the microwave, stirring often, until smooth, about 10 seconds. Dip the large end of an acorn caramel into the melted chocolate to cover about 1/4 inch. Allow any excess chocolate to drip off. While the acorn is still wet, dip the chocolate end into the jimmies to coat. Transfer to the cookie sheet. Repeat with the remaining acorns. Refrigerate until set, about 5 minutes.

4. Spoon 1/4 cup of the chocolate frosting into a ziplock bag, press out the excess air, and seal. Spread the tops of the cupcakes with the remaining chocolate frosting and smooth. Arrange the cupcakes in pairs to make a circle on a large platter.

5. Gently press the leaves into the frosting on the cupcakes, overlapping them. The leaves on the edge of the right half of the wreath will sweep to the right, while those on the left half will sweep to the left. Place the acorns randomly over the cupcakes. Snip a 1/8-inch corner from the bag with the chocolate frosting and pipe a dot of frosting at the top of each acorn to make a stem.

LARRY THE TURKEY

Larry the Turkey does double duty at Thanksgiving, letting Larry know where to sit at the beginning of the meal and providing a dessert for him at the end. A delicious combination of pumpkin cupcakes, caramel frosting, and ginger cookies, this turkey will be gobbled up in no time. Of course, the best part is naming each turkey and hearing the kids scream, "Hey, look, everybody, Uncle Larry's a turkey!"

24 standard Pumpkin Spice cupcakes (page 219) baked in white paper liners

24 mini Pumpkin Spice cupcakes (page 219) baked in white paper liners

1 cup vanilla frosting

1/2 cup chocolate frosting

24 thin ginger-flavored scalloped cookies (Anna's Ginger Thins)

2 cups candy corn

1 1/2 cups caramel jimmies

1 can (16 ounces) plus 1 cup caramel frosting

24 pieces Indian candy corn

48 brown chocolate-covered sunflower seeds (available at gourmet candy stores or see Sources, page 229)

1 roll red fruit leather (Fruit by the Foot)

24 graham cracker sticks (Honey Maid Graham Sticks)

12 marshmallows

1. Spoon the vanilla and chocolate frosting into separate ziplock bags, press out the excess air, and seal. Snip a $1/8$-inch corner from the bag with the vanilla frosting and pipe a dot of frosting on 7 adjacent scallops on each ginger cookie to make the tail fan. Add a piece of candy corn to each dot of frosting, pointed end facing in (see photo, page 184).

2. Place the caramel jimmies in a small shallow bowl. Spread the caramel frosting on top of all the cupcakes, standard and mini, and smooth. Roll the edge of the standard cupcakes in the jimmies (see page 12). Dip the top edge of the mini cupcakes in the jimmies.

3. Press 1 piece of Indian candy corn into the center of each mini cupcake, flat side down, for the beak. Pipe 2 dots of the vanilla frosting above the beak for the eyes and insert 2 brown sunflower seeds, pointed end down. Cut the red fruit leather into twenty-four $1\frac{1}{2}$-inch-long teardrop shapes and lay them over the beak to make the wattle.

4. Snip a $1/8$-inch corner from the bag with the chocolate frosting and pipe names on the flat side of the graham cracker cookies.

5. Enlarge the hole in the corner of the bag with the chocolate frosting to $1/4$ inch. Using clean scissors, cut the marshmallows in half on the diagonal. Place 1 marshmallow half, cut side down, near the edge of one of the standard cupcakes, with the tapered end facing the center, to make a support for the tail. Pipe a dot of chocolate frosting on the tapered end. Place the tail cookie on the marshmallow, pressing the undecorated edge into the frosting on the marshmallow. Add the mini cupcake head on top so that half of it is resting on the undecorated edge of the cookie and the other half is pressed lightly into the frosting to secure.

6. Add the graham cookies at the base of the mini cupcakes, securing with a dot of frosting.

7. Arrange the turkeys on the table as place cards. Place 2 candy corns on the table in front of each turkey to make the feet.

Holiday on Icing

Every year the holiday season gets crazier. Join the madness by swallowing a string of glittering lights, baking a family of snowmen, or serving your guests a platter of shiny decorative ornaments. These cupcakes make festive desserts, madcap party treats, and special gifts that won't be exchanged.

EDIBLE ORNAMENTS

These ornaments are a press-and-play project: there's nothing more to it than pressing candies into the frosting. No piping fancy designs, no complicated shaping, and nothing to melt. Simply frost the cupcakes, roll them in sugar, choose colorful and graphic candies, and press them into your own beautiful designs. Make a batch for a holiday dessert or put them in mini gift boxes for a sweet party favor or take-along gift.

8 vanilla cupcakes baked in red paper liners (see
   Sources, page 229)
8 vanilla cupcakes baked in green paper liners (see
   Sources)
8 vanilla cupcakes baked in white paper liners

2 cans (12 ounces each) whipped vanilla frosting
$1/2$ cup each green, light green, red, yellow, and white
   decorating sugars (available at baking supply stores
   or see Sources)
24 yellow spice drops
   Black licorice laces, cut into twenty-four $1^1/_4$-inch
   pieces
24 thin pretzel sticks
   Assortment of colored fruit chews and fruit leather
   (Laffy Taffys, Airheads, Starbursts, Fruit by the Foot)
   Red licorice laces (Twizzlers Pull-n-Peel)
1 cup mini candy-coated chocolates (M&M's Minis)
   Cinnamon Red Hots or candy decors

1. Spoon $1/2$ cup of the vanilla frosting into a ziplock bag, press out the excess air, seal, and set aside.

2. Place the decorating sugars in separate small shallow bowls. Spread the tops of all the cupcakes with the vanilla frosting, mounding it slightly (see page 11). Starting at the edge, roll the top of each cupcake in one of the sugars to coat completely.

3. To make the top of the ornament, use a round toothpick to poke a hole in each end of one of the spice drops. Bend one of the black licorice pieces in half and insert both ends into the hole in the bottom of the spice drop to make a loop. Insert one end of a pretzel stick into the hole in the rounded top of the spice drop, pushing it in about 1/2 inch. Press the other end of the pretzel all the way into one of the cupcakes. Repeat with the remaining cupcakes.

4. Roll out the fruit chews on a piece of wax paper to 1/8 inch thick. Use a pastry wheel, clean craft scissors, or regular scissors to cut the fruit chews and fruit leather into decorative pieces. Arrange the fruit-chew pieces, fruit leather, and red laces on top of the cupcakes to make stripes, bands, and lines. Snip a 1/8-inch corner from the bag with the vanilla frosting and pipe dots in different patterns over the cupcakes and on top of the fruit chews. Press the chocolate candies, Cinnamon Red Hots, and candy decors into the frosting to secure.

5. Set the cupcakes in another paper liner and place in small boxes or on a serving platter.

STRING OF D'LIGHTS

The bulbs of this string of lights are cut from graham crackers, then frosted and rolled in colored sugar. The green licorice and dots make the cord, and the old-fashioned plug is crafted from Chiclets and a large gumdrop.

12 vanilla cupcakes baked in green paper liners (see
   Sources, page 229)

12 whole honey graham crackers

 1 can (16 ounces) vanilla frosting

$\frac{1}{4}$ cup each red, green, blue, white, orange, and yellow
   decorating sugars (available at baking supply stores
   or see Sources)

12 green gumdrops (Dots)

12 thin pretzel sticks

 1 package green licorice laces, cut into 6- or 7-inch
   double-strand lengths (available at candy stores or
   see Sources)

 2 pieces of white mint gum (Chiclets, Eclipse)

 1 large green gumdrop

1. Using a serrated knife, trim the graham crackers following the template (page 192). Spread a thin layer of the vanilla frosting on top of the cupcakes. Position one trimmed graham cracker on top of each cupcake, pressing it into the frosting to secure it (the narrow end of the graham cracker should extend over the edge of the cupcake slightly).

2. Place the decorating sugars in separate small shallow bowls. Spoon the remaining vanilla frosting into a ziplock bag, press out the excess air, and seal. Snip a $\frac{1}{4}$-inch corner from the bag. Working on 1 cupcake at a time, pipe the

frosting on top and sides of the cracker to mound slightly. Spread the top of the frosting to smooth. Roll the top of the frosted cracker in one of the colored sugars to cover completely. Repeat with the remaining cupcakes.

3. Use a round toothpick to poke a hole in the rounded top of the 12 gumdrops. Insert a pretzel stick into the rounded top of one of the 12 green gumdrops, pushing it in about $\frac{1}{2}$ inch. Use a round toothpick to make a hole on each side of the gumdrop and insert the end of a green licorice lace into one side. Insert another licorice lace in the other side. Continue connecting the 12 gumdrops. Press the 2 pieces of gum into the flat end of the large gumdrop and press one end of a green licorice lace into the rounded top to make the plug. Pinch together several lengths of licorice lace to make the electric cord longer and be sure to connect it to the final gumdrop in the series.

4. Arrange the cupcakes on a serving platter with the larger ends of the sugared crackers facing one another. Insert the pretzel end of each gumdrop assembly into a cupcake under the wide end of the cracker. Twist the licorice laces between the cupcakes to make the cord slightly tangled.

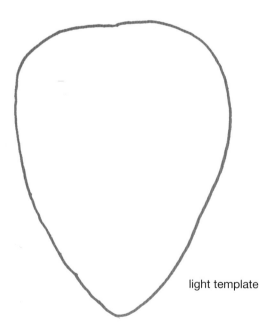

light template

SNOW GLOBES

Shake it, shake it, baby . . . Expect blizzards of fun when you decorate jumbo cupcakes with snowy scenes and place them on a base made from a chocolate-covered cracker.

6 jumbo vanilla or chocolate cupcakes baked in silver foil liners

1 can (16 ounces) vanilla frosting
  Green food coloring

2 tablespoons chocolate frosting

3/4 cup white coarse decorating sugar (available at baking supply stores or see Sources, page 229)

2 tablespoons snowflake decors (available at baking supply stores or see Sources)

1 tablespoon blue nonpareils (available at baking supply stores or see Sources)

12 chocolate-covered graham crackers (Keebler)

1. Tint 1/2 cup of the vanilla frosting green with the food coloring and spoon it into a ziplock bag. Spoon 2 tablespoons of the vanilla frosting into a small ziplock bag. Spoon the chocolate frosting into a small ziplock bag. Press out the excess air in the bags of frosting and seal.

2. Spoon the decorating sugar into a small shallow bowl. Spread the remaining vanilla frosting on top of the cupcakes and smooth. Roll the edge of each cupcake in the sugar (see page 12). Sprinkle the top of the cupcakes with some of the snowflake decors and blue nonpareils.

HOUSE

Makes 2 jumbo cupcakes

1 whole graham cracker

1 strip red sour straw (Sour Punch Straws)

1 each red and green fruit chews (Jolly Ranchers,
   Starbursts, Tootsie Fruit Rolls)

1 chocolate taffy (Tootsie Roll)

Using a serrated knife and following the house template, cut the graham cracker into 2 house shapes. Press the house crackers into the frosting on 2 of the cupcakes, with the peak toward the center and the flat side at the bottom edge of the cupcake. Cut the red sour straw into four 2$^{1}/_{2}$-inch lengths for the roof and place 2 pieces along the roofline of each graham cracker house, allowing the red straw to overhang slightly on both sides. Roll out the red and green fruit chews on a sheet of wax paper to $^{1}/_{8}$ inch thick. Cut the fruit chews into four $^{1}/_{4}$-inch squares for the windows and two $^{1}/_{2}$-by-$^{1}/_{3}$-inch rectangles for the doors. Cut 2 small chimneys from the chocolate taffy and add one to each roof. Snip a $^{1}/_{8}$-inch corner from the bags with the vanilla, green, and chocolate frosting. Pipe 3 dots of vanilla frosting on each graham cracker house and attach the windows and doors. Using the green frosting, pipe bushes at the base of the house. Using the squeeze-and-pull technique (see page 15), pipe vanilla-frosting icicles along the bottom of the roof. Add a dot of chocolate frosting for the doorknob. Add several dots of vanilla frosting to the house and press a few snowflake decors and blue nonpareils into the frosting.

TREE

Makes 2 jumbo cupcakes

1 chocolate taffy (Tootsie Roll)
2 small yellow star candies (candy necklace)

Cut the chocolate taffy into two $^{1}/_{2}$-by-1-inch pieces. Press 1 piece into the frosting at the bottom edge of each cupcake for the tree trunk. To make the tree, pipe a 1$^{1}/_{2}$-inch-wide row of vertical lines of green frosting across the top of the tree trunk, squeezing and pulling each line into a long downward point. Pipe the next row above and overlapping the first. Continue piping in this way, each row smaller than the last, to make a tree shape. Sprinkle a few snowflake decors and nonpareils on the trees. Top each tree with a yellow star candy.

SNOWMAN

Makes 2 jumbo cupcakes

2 large white spice drops
1 orange spice drop
2 black licorice gumdrops (Crows)
Black licorice laces (available at candy stores or see Sources, page 229)

6 red round sprinkles (available at baking supply stores
   or see Sources)

1. Cut each white spice drop in half crosswise. Roll out the bottom half to make a disk that is slightly larger in diameter than the top half. For the body of each snowman, press the flattened disk at the bottom edge of the cupcake, cut side down. Place the top half of the spice drop, cut side down, above the disk to make the head. Cut the orange spice drop into 2 small triangle noses and attach 1 to each head with a small dot of vanilla frosting.

2. Trim each licorice gumdrop into a $1/2$-inch square to make the hat. Cut two $3/4$-inch pieces of licorice lace for the hat brims and press 1 into the frosting above the head on each cupcake. Add a square of licorice to make the hat. Pipe a green-frosting scarf across the neck, where the head touches the body. Add 3 dots of vanilla frosting down the middle of the snowman and attach the red sprinkles for the buttons. Using the chocolate frosting, pipe eyes and mouth. Add a few snowflake decors and blue nonpareils.

TO ASSEMBLE

For each cupcake, arrange 2 chocolate-covered graham crackers, side by side, on a serving plate. Pipe a dollop of vanilla frosting on top of the cookies. Place the cupcake on its side on the cookies, with the decorations upright.

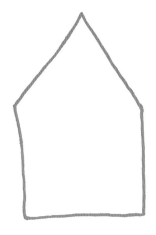

house template

GINGERBREAD BOYS

Gingerbread and chocolate are two of our favorite things, so what could be better than combining them in these delicious gingerbread boys? Our Next-to-Instant Ganache (page 226), made by zapping store-bought icing in the microwave, produces the sophisticated candy-coated sheen. It may take a little practice to bridge the gaps between the cupcakes with the white-frosting outline, but if the line breaks, just go back and start piping again. The still-soft frosting will melt into itself and heal the break.

21 Orange Spice cupcakes or Gingerbread (page 219)
    baked in brown paper liners (see Sources, page 229)

1 cup vanilla frosting
1 can (16 ounces) milk chocolate frosting
3 each red, green, and yellow spice drops
6 green candy-coated chocolates (M&M's)

1. Spoon the vanilla frosting into a ziplock bag, press out the excess air, and seal. Spoon the chocolate frosting into a 2-cup microwavable glass bowl or measuring cup. Microwave the chocolate frosting, stirring frequently, until it is the texture of lightly whipped cream (see page 18), 20 to 30 seconds. Working with 1 cupcake at a time, hold the cupcake by its paper liner and dip it into the frosting just up to the edge of the liner. Hold the cupcake above the surface and allow the excess frosting to drip off. Turn the cupcake right side up and place on a cookie sheet. Repeat with the remaining cupcakes. If the frosting begins to thicken, reheat in the microwave for several seconds, stirring well.

2. Arrange 7 cupcakes on a serving platter or cookie sheet to make a gingerbread boy, making sure the cupcakes lightly touch one another: 3 cupcakes in a vertical row for the head and body, 2 on either side of the bottom cupcake for the

feet, and 2 on either side of the second cupcake for the hands (see photo, page 199). Repeat to make 2 more gingerbread boys.

3. Snip a ⅛-inch corner from the bag with the vanilla frosting. Pipe an outline of the gingerbread boy along the outer edge of each cupcake group. Pipe 3 dots of vanilla frosting down the center of the body and add the spice drops to make the buttons. Pipe 2 dots for the eyes and add the green chocolate candies. Pipe a mouth.

PARTRIDGE IN A PEAR TREE

Using almonds for the plumage gives this partridge a sophisticated look.
It's so pretty, you may be tempted to keep it as a decoration all season.
Make two, one for eating and one to deck the halls.

10 vanilla cupcakes baked in green paper liners (see
    Sources, page 229)

27 chocolate taffy pieces (Tootsie Rolls)
 1 can (16 ounces) plus 1 cup vanilla frosting
   Green and yellow food coloring
 1 plain mini doughnut
 1 thin chocolate cookie (Famous Chocolate Wafers)
 1 package (10 ounces) sliced almonds
 2 mini chocolate chips
 1 tablespoon unsalted hulled sunflower seeds
 1 brown chocolate-covered sunflower seed (available
    at gourmet candy stores or see Sources)

1. Unwrap the chocolate taffy pieces. Working with 3 pieces of chocolate taffy at
   a time, microwave for 2 to 3 seconds to soften slightly. Press 3 of the pieces together to form into a pear shape. Continue until you have 8 pears. Shape 2 of
   the chocolate taffy pieces into a 1$\frac{1}{2}$-inch ball to be used as the partridge's
   head. Cut the remaining piece of taffy crosswise into 9 thin strips, about $\frac{1}{2}$ inch
   long. Form 1 piece into a teardrop shape for the top crest of the partridge; form
   the remaining 8 pieces into stems for the pears.

2. Spoon $\frac{1}{4}$ cup of the vanilla frosting into a ziplock bag, press out the excess air,
   and seal. Spoon 1 cup of the vanilla frosting into a 1-cup glass measuring cup.
   Tint the remaining vanilla frosting bright green with the food coloring, spoon
   into a ziplock bag, press out the excess air, and seal. Snip a $\frac{1}{8}$-inch corner
   from the bags with the green and vanilla frosting. Attach the pears with a dot of

green frosting to 8 of the cupcakes, positioning each pear off to one side. Attach the mini doughnut to the top of one of the remaining cupcakes with a dot of vanilla frosting. Add the ball-shaped taffy head to one side on top of the doughnut and secure with vanilla frosting. Place the 8 pear cupcakes and the partridge cupcake in the freezer for 10 minutes.

3. Using a serrated knife, cut the chocolate cookie into a 2-by-2-by-1¼-inch triangle to make the tail (see page 20). Sort through the sliced almonds and pick out all the brown end pieces and the nicest-looking slices.

4. When the cupcakes are slightly frozen, microwave the 1 cup of vanilla frosting for 10- to 15-second intervals, stirring frequently, until the frosting is the consistency of lightly whipped cream (see page 18).

5. Holding the partridge cupcake by its paper liner, dip it into the melted frosting just to the bottom of the doughnut. Hold the cupcake above the surface and allow the excess frosting to drip off (see page 19). Carefully invert the cupcake and place it on a cookie sheet.

6. Tint the remaining melted frosting yellow with the food coloring, stirring well to blend. If the frosting becomes too thick, reheat in the microwave for several seconds, stirring well. Holding one of the pear cupcakes by its paper liner, dip it into the yellow frosting just to cover the pear. Allow the excess frosting to drip off. Carefully turn the cupcake right side up and place it on the cookie sheet. Repeat with the remaining 7 pear-topped cupcakes.

7. Working on one cupcake at a time, pipe lines of green frosting around the edge using the squeeze-and-release technique to make the grass (see page 15). Continue working inward in concentric circles, each row overlapping the previous row, until the top of the cupcake is covered. Repeat with the remaining cupcakes; one cupcake will have only the grass on it.

8. For the wings, pipe vanilla frosting on both sides of the frosted doughnut and arrange 3 horizontal rows of almond slices, overlapping them slightly. To make the tail, use some of the vanilla frosting to attach the chocolate cookie triangle, pointed end down, on the side opposite the head. Starting at the pointed end of the cookie, add the brown end pieces of almonds, as the feathers, securing them with the vanilla frosting and overlapping them slightly. Add 2 or 3 rows of the brown end pieces on top of the partridge's head, overlapping them slightly.

Pipe a small dot of vanilla frosting for each eye patch and add a brown end piece of almond horizontally. Pipe a dot of vanilla frosting on the eye patch and add the chocolate chip, flat side out, for the eye. Pipe a white highlight on each eye. To make the ruff, use dots of vanilla frosting to attach the hulled sunflower seeds, pointed ends in, in 2 overlapping rows across the chest. Use a round toothpick to make a small hole in the top of the head and in the top of each pear. Insert the narrow end of the teardrop-shaped taffy crest in the hole on top of the head and insert the taffy stems in the top of the pears. Use a dot of vanilla frosting to attach the chocolate-covered sunflower seed for the beak.

9. Place the green-frosted cupcake without a pear in the center of a serving platter. Arrange 4 pear cupcakes around the center cupcake, pears facing out. Arrange the remaining 4 pear cupcakes on top of the first layer of cupcakes, pears facing out, close together. Place the partridge cupcake in the center on top of the green-frosted cupcake.

NUTCRACKERS SWEET

These nutcrackers may appear a little daunting, but they are actually simple to make. Instead of looking at the whole, examine each cupcake; none of the individual designs is difficult.

Get everything in place—cupcakes, frosting, candies, cookies—and gather your tools before starting. The French call this *mise en place;* we call it common sense.

18 vanilla cupcakes baked in white paper liners

2 cans (16 ounces each) vanilla frosting
  Red and yellow food coloring

1/4 cup dark chocolate frosting

1/2 cup each red, blue, and green decorating sugars (available at baking supply stores or see Sources, page 229)

3 Pirouette cookies (Pepperidge Farm French Vanilla)

1 tablespoon light corn syrup

6 white and 3 pink gumballs

6 thin chocolate cookies (Famous Chocolate Wafers)

2 pink and 3 white candy wafers (Necco)

6 blue mini candy-coated chocolates (M&M's Minis)

6 chocolate-covered almonds

9 dark-chocolate-covered cookies (Cadbury Dark Chocolate Fingers)

9 yellow candy-coated chocolates (M&M's)

27 yellow mini candy-coated chocolates (M&M's Minis)

1. Tint 1/2 cup of the vanilla frosting pale pink with the red food coloring. Tint 1/4 cup of the vanilla frosting yellow with the food coloring and spoon into a ziplock bag. Press out the excess air and seal the bag. Spoon the dark chocolate frost-

ing and ¹/₂ cup of the vanilla frosting into separate ziplock bags, press out the excess air, seal, and set aside.

2. Line a cookie sheet with wax paper. Spoon each color of decorating sugar into a separate small shallow bowl. Using a serrated knife, cut each Pirouette cookie crosswise into two 2-inch pieces. Heat the corn syrup in a small bowl in the microwave until boiling, about 5 seconds. Working on 2 cookie pieces at a time, make the arms by brushing the cookies with the warm corn syrup and rolling them in the same color of sugar to cover completely. Snip a ¹/₈-inch corner from the bag with the vanilla frosting. Pipe a dot of frosting at one end of each arm and attach the white gumballs to make the hands. Place on the cookie sheet and let set for about 30 minutes.

3. Using a serrated knife and angling it slightly inward toward the bottom, cut ¹/₄ inch from opposite sides of 3 of the thin chocolate cookies to make the hats. Cut ¹/₂ inch from opposite sides of 2 of the remaining cookies to make the brims. Trim ¹/₄ inch from each end of the brim. Cut the remaining chocolate cookie into 6 pie-shaped pieces to use as support for the hair. Cut the 2 pink candy wafers in half. Trim ¹/₈ inch from opposite sides of the 3 white candy wafers to make the mouths. Cut the pink gumballs in half for the cheeks.

4. Spread the tops of 3 of the cupcakes with the pink frosting to make the heads. Insert 1 pink wafer half vertically, rounded edge up, into the center of each cupcake to make the nose. Add 2 halved pink gumballs on either side of the nose for the cheeks. Add 1 white wafer, trimmed edges horizontal, about ¹/₄ inch down from the nose to make the mouth. Insert the pointed end of 2 of the pie-shaped cookie pieces on either side of each cupcake to support the hair.

5. Spread vanilla frosting on top of 6 of the cupcakes and smooth. Spread the tops of the remaining 9 cupcakes with the vanilla frosting, mounding it slightly (see page 11). Starting at the edge, roll the tops of the 9 mounded cupcakes in the colored sugars, 3 in each color.

6. To assemble the nutcrackers, place 2 sugared cupcakes of the same color side by side on a serving platter. Place 1 sugared cupcake of the same color underneath, touching the other two. Place 1 pink-frosted cupcake head above the 2 sugared cupcakes and add 1 vanilla-frosted cupcake above that for the hat. Place 1 vanilla-frosted cupcake below the 2 sugared cupcakes for the feet (see photo). Repeat with the other cupcakes to make 3 nutcrackers.

7. Snip a $1/16$-inch corner from the bags with the chocolate and yellow frosting. Pipe a dot of vanilla frosting on either side of the 2 sugared cupcakes that form the chest. Attach the sugared cookie arms, matching the color to the cupcakes, with the gumball ends pointing down.

8. Pipe dots of vanilla frosting for the eyes and add the blue chocolate candies. Using the chocolate frosting, pipe pupils on the eyes and a line above each eye for the eyelids. Pipe teeth on the white-wafer mouth with the chocolate frosting. Increase the size of the cut corner on the bag with the chocolate frosting to $1/8$-inch and pipe eyebrows and a mustache. To make the hair, start at the edge of the cupcake where one of the cookie supports is inserted and pipe lines of vanilla frosting from the cupcake onto the cookie support to cover it completely. Pipe another row just above and slightly overlapping the first, squeezing and pulling the frosting away from the cupcake (see the fur technique on page 15). Repeat on the other side. To make the beard, start about 1 inch below the mouth, on the sugar-coated chest, and pipe a row of 2 or 3 vertical lines of vanilla frosting. Pipe a second row above and slightly overlapping the first, widening it with an extra line of frosting. The third row is piped from the edge of the cupcake and is slightly wider again, creating a tapered goatee.

9. Place the trimmed hat cookie on the cupcake above the head, with the tapered end at the bottom. Press the trimmed cookie piece for the brim, cut edge down into the frosting at the top of the head, directly below the hat.

10. Arrange the chocolate almonds at the lower edge of the bottom cupcake, narrow ends in, for the feet. Trim 2 chocolate-covered cookies to fit vertically, side by side, on the bottom cupcake for the boots. Place a whole chocolate-covered cookie horizontally between the rows of sugared cupcakes for the belt.

11. Pipe diagonal lines of yellow frosting on the hat and chest. Pipe a yellow fringe around the top of each sugared-cookie arm and add a regular yellow chocolate candy to make epaulets. Pipe 3 dots along either side of the diagonal lines on the chest and attach yellow mini chocolate candies for buttons. Add a yellow mini candy at the top of the hat where the lines of yellow frosting meet. Pipe 2 yellow dots of frosting at the top of the cookie boots and attach yellow mini candies. Pipe a yellow dot of frosting in the center of the belt and attach a regular yellow chocolate candy for the belt buckle.

FROSTING THE SNOWMEN

This is one cool family that should never go to Florida. The supersized snowmen are made by stacking mini and standard cupcakes.

9 standard vanilla cupcakes baked in white paper liners
7 mini vanilla cupcakes baked in white paper liners

1 can (16 ounces) plus 1/2 cup vanilla frosting
  Green, black, and yellow food coloring (available at baking supply stores or see Sources, page 229)
1 cup flaked sweetened coconut
3 orange carrot-shaped hard candies (available at candy stores or see Sources)
6 mini chocolate chips
1 pink, 1 blue, 2 green, 2 red, and 3 yellow fruit chews (Tootsie Fruit Rolls, Laffy Taffys, Starbursts, Airheads)
1 mini and 1 regular chocolate cream-filled sandwich cookie (Oreos)
2 pink candy-coated chocolates (M&M's)
1 heart-shaped hard candy (Runts)
4 green spice drops

1. Tint 1 cup of the vanilla frosting dark green with the food coloring and spoon it into a ziplock bag. Press out the excess air and seal the bag. Tint 1 tablespoon each of the vanilla frosting black and yellow with the food coloring. Spoon each color into a separate small ziplock bag, press out the excess air, and seal.

2. Place the coconut in a shallow bowl. Spread the tops of 5 of the standard and 3 of the mini cupcakes with the remaining vanilla frosting and smooth. Roll the

edges of the frosted cupcakes in the coconut (see page 12). Using 4 of the standard frosted cupcakes, make 2 stacks of 2 cupcakes.

3. Insert the orange candy in the center of the 3 mini vanilla-frosted cupcakes to make noses. Add 2 mini chocolate chips, pointed end in, to make the eyes. Snip a 1/8-inch corner from the bags with the black and yellow frosting. Pipe black dots under the orange nose to make the mouth. Place 2 of the mini cupcake heads on their sides on top of the stacked cupcakes. Place the remaining mini cupcake on its side on top of the remaining frosted standard cupcake.

4. Roll out the colored fruit chews on a sheet of wax paper to 1/8 inch thick. Using the 5 templates (page 212) as guides, cut out the tie, scarf, waistband, apron, and earmuffs. For the striped hat, cut thin strips of the red and yellow fruit chews and place them side by side, alternating the colors, on a sheet of wax paper. Reroll to press together. Following the hat template, cut out the hat and press together to create a cone shape. Separate the halves of the regular chocolate sandwich cookie and remove the cream from the center. Use a dot of black frosting to attach the mini chocolate sandwich cookie to the outer surface of one of the cookie halves to make the hat. Add the scarf, tie, apron with waistband, hats, and earmuffs to the cupcakes, using a dot of vanilla frosting to secure them if necessary. Attach 1 pink chocolate candy at the bottom of the earmuffs on each side with a dot of vanilla frosting. Add the heart-shaped candy to the snow mother using a dot of vanilla frosting to secure.

5. Reinforce a bottom corner of the ziplock bag with the green frosting, using 6 overlapping layers of Scotch tape. Pinch the taped corner flat, then snip a small M-shape in the corner to make a star tip (see page 14).

6. Pipe a dot of green frosting at the center of each of the remaining 4 mini cupcakes. Press the spice drops, flat side down, into the frosting. Pipe the green frosting around the edge of the mini cupcakes and the remaining 4 standard cupcakes, then work inward in concentric circles, always pulling the frosting away from the center and slightly overlapping the rows, until the cupcake is completely covered (see page 15). Stack the green-frosted cupcakes at different heights to make the trees.

7. Arrange the snow people and tree cupcakes on a serving platter.

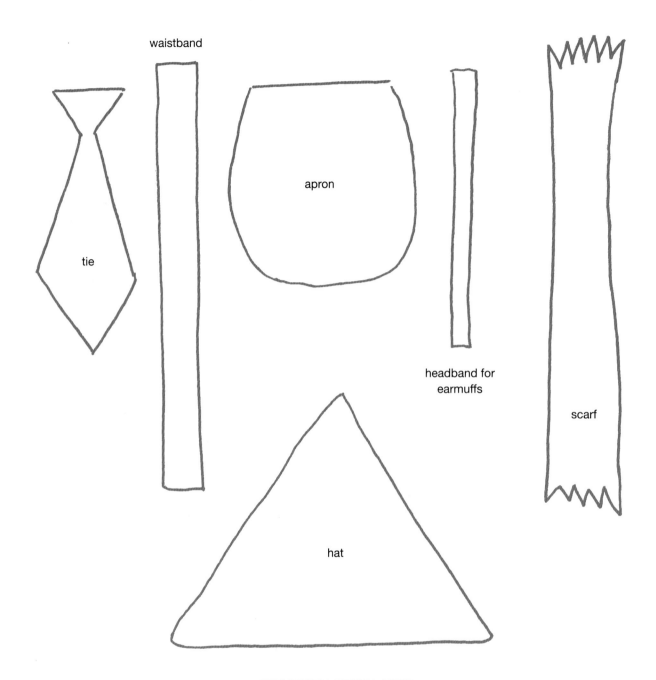

waistband

apron

tie

headband for
earmuffs

scarf

hat

SNOWMEN TEMPLATES

WHITE WREATH

This elegant holiday wreath will have your guests dreaming of a white Christmas. It is created using the same chocolate-paint technique used for Autumn Leaves and Wedding Cake, except the melting wafers here are white chocolate and the leaves are mint. You can add even more winter freshness by decorating your wreath with crushed peppermint sticks. The holly berries are candy-coated chocolates, but any round red candy of the appropriate size will work. Adjust the size of the wreath to match your party, and if you have extra cupcakes, cover them with additional white chocolate leaves and red candies and place them around the table as decorations.

12 vanilla cupcakes baked in silver foil liners

2 bunches fresh mint, preferably with large leaves

1½ cups white chocolate melting wafers (available at
      baking supply stores or see Sources, page 229)

1 can (16 ounces) vanilla frosting

1 cup white coarse decorating sugar (available at
      baking supply stores or see Sources)

1 cup red candy-coated milk chocolate balls (Cadbury)

1 decorative ribbon

1. Line 2 cookie sheets with wax paper. Pick the mint leaves from the stems. Wash and pat dry on paper towels.

2. Place the white chocolate melting wafers in a medium microwavable bowl. Microwave, stirring frequently, until the chocolate is smooth, about 1 minute.

3. Using a small, clean craft brush or your fingertip, coat the top side of each mint leaf with an even layer of the melted chocolate (see page 159). Transfer to one

of the cookie sheets, chocolate side up, and allow the leaf to bend and curve slightly. Repeat with the remaining mint leaves to make about 75 leaves. If the chocolate becomes too thick, reheat in the microwave for several seconds, stirring well. Place the leaves in the refrigerator until set, about 5 minutes.

4. Carefully peel the leaves from the hardened chocolate. They come off surprisingly easily. Use a toothpick or clean tweezers to remove any small pieces of mint leaf that may remain. (The leaves can be made up to 5 days in advance, covered, and kept in a cool dry place.)

5. Spoon $1/4$ cup of the vanilla frosting into a ziplock bag, press out the excess air, and seal. Spoon the decorating sugar into a small shallow bowl. Spread the tops of the cupcakes with the remaining vanilla frosting and smooth. Roll the edges of the cupcakes in the sugar (see page 12). Arrange the cupcakes, close together, in a circle on a large platter.

6. Press the chocolate leaves into the cupcakes oriented in one direction to cover the cupcakes. Snip a $1/8$-inch corner from the bag with the vanilla frosting and pipe dots of frosting randomly on the leaves to attach the red candies. Sprinkle the platter with the remaining decorative sugar. Tie a decorative ribbon into a bow and place on the platter.

Cupcakes and Frostings

Our cupcakes made from doctored store-bought mix stand up to homemade versions in taste test after taste test. We use buttermilk to cut the edge of the sweetness and give the cake homemade flavor, and we add an egg to improve the structure. Cupcakes made from this variation on store-bought mixes cook up evenly without sinkholes or soft spots in the middle, and you get a nice firm surface that doesn't pull apart when you start frosting.

But for special occasions like dinner parties or weddings, we prefer homemade cupcakes. The ones in this chapter bake up beautifully and are delicious additions to any special event.

Any cake tastes best the day it is baked. But when we are short on time, we make the cupcakes the night before, wrap them in plastic and decorate them the next day. Both the ones from the improved box mix and the homemade kind stay moist overnight.

We have yet to find a homemade frosting that can do what a store-bought one does. That's why we use store-bought frosting right out of the can for most of our projects. Canned frosting is both smooth and elastic. Squeeze and pull a ziplock bag filled with store-bought frosting, and it delivers an elegant shape time after time. Most store-bought frostings also tint easily, resulting in vibrant colors. And, as if all that weren't enough, store-bought frosting holds up to the heat, melting into a consistently smooth texture for dipping.

While you can't beat store-bought frosting for shaping, tinting, and dipping, the flavor of homemade frosting is superior. You may want to make the frosting from scratch when you are working on a project in which the frosting doesn't do much design work, but simply serves to hold the candies together, or when texture, brilliant color, and melting are not an issue, or when you are preparing for an extra-fancy occasion, like a wedding, or whenever taste should trump texture.

A couple of our frostings are a combination of store-bought and homemade. Next-to-Instant Ganache, which is simply microwaved store-bought chocolate frosting, gives cupcakes a beautiful smooth coating. Almost-Homemade Vanilla Buttercream uses off-the-shelf Marshmallow Fluff and results in a buttercream that rivals the real thing.

PERFECT CAKE-MIX CUPCAKES

You can use any standard cake mix, but avoid those with pudding in the mix and steer clear of lighter cake mixes such as angel food, since cupcake projects need a firm cake that will hold up when it's decorated. If you don't have buttermilk on hand, you can make a fair substitution by adding 1 tablespoon lemon juice to 1 cup whole milk. Let it sit for 10 minutes to sour. (Actual buttermilk is better.)

1 **box (18.25 ounces) cake mix (French vanilla, devil's food, or yellow)**
1 **cup buttermilk (in place of the water called for on the box)**
 Vegetable oil (the amount on the box)
4 **large eggs (in place of the number called for on the box)**

1. Preheat the oven to 350°F. Line 24 muffin cups with paper liners.

2. Follow the box instructions, putting all the ingredients in a large bowl and using the buttermilk in place of the water specified (the box will call for more water than the amount of buttermilk that you are using), using the amount of vegetable oil that is called for (typically, white or yellow cakes call for $^1/_3$ cup; the chocolate cakes usually call for $^1/_2$ cup), and adding the eggs. Beat with an electric mixer until moistened, about 30 seconds. Increase the speed to high and beat until thick, 2 minutes longer.

3. Spoon half of the batter into a ziplock bag. Snip a $^1/_4$-inch corner from the bag and fill the paper liners two-thirds full (see page 9). Repeat with the remaining batter. Bake until golden and a toothpick inserted in the center comes out clean, 15 to 20 minutes. Remove the cupcakes from the baking pans, place on a wire rack, and allow to cool completely.

PUMPKIN SPICE

1 box (18.25 ounces) French vanilla or
  yellow cake mix
1 cup canned pumpkin
1 teaspoon pumpkin pie spice
$^3/_4$ cup buttermilk
$^1/_3$ cup vegetable oil
4 large eggs

    Make as directed.

CHOCOLATE CHUNK SURPRISE

1 box (18.25 ounces) devil's food cake
  mix
1 cup buttermilk
$^1/_2$ cup vegetable oil
4 large eggs
24 caramel cream–filled chocolates
  (Milky Way Miniatures)

    Make as directed, adding a caramel
cream–filled chocolate to each muffin
cup filled with batter.

CHOCOLATE MINT

1 box (18.25 ounces) devil's food cake
  mix
1 cup buttermilk
$^1/_2$ cup vegetable oil
4 large eggs
$^3/_4$ cup chopped mint chocolates
  (Andes Crème de Menthe Thins)

    Make as directed, folding the chopped
mint chocolates into the batter.

ORANGE SPICE

1 box (18.25 ounces) French vanilla or
  yellow cake mix
1 cup buttermilk
$^1/_3$ cup vegetable oil
4 large eggs
2 teaspoons pumpkin pie spice
$^1/_2$ teaspoon grated orange peel

    Make as directed, folding the pump-
kin pie spice and orange peel into the
batter.

BANANA CHOCOLATE

1 box (18.25 ounces) devil's food cake
  mix
1 cup mashed bananas (about 3
  medium)
$^3/_4$ cup buttermilk
$^1/_2$ cup vegetable oil
4 large eggs

    Make as directed.

GINGERBREAD

1 box (18.25 ounces) French vanilla or
  yellow cake mix
$^1/_2$ cup buttermilk
$^1/_2$ cup molasses
$^1/_3$ cup vegetable oil
4 large eggs
1$^1/_2$ teaspoons ground ginger
$^1/_2$ teaspoon cinnamon
$^1/_4$ teaspoon nutmeg

    Make as directed.

OUR FAVORITE HOMEMADE CUPCAKES

CHOCOLATE CUPCAKES
Makes 16 standard cupcakes or 12 standard and 12 mini cupcakes

1³/₄ cups all-purpose flour
¹/₄ cup unsweetened cocoa powder
³/₄ teaspoon baking soda
¹/₂ teaspoon baking powder
¹/₂ teaspoon salt
1¹/₂ sticks (12 tablespoons) unsalted butter, softened
³/₄ cup lightly packed brown sugar
2 large eggs
2 ounces unsweetened chocolate, melted
1 cup buttermilk
1 teaspoon vanilla extract

1. Preheat the oven to 350°F. Line the muffin cups with paper liners.

2. Whisk together the flour, cocoa powder, baking soda, baking powder, and salt in a medium bowl. In another medium bowl, with an electric mixer on high, beat the butter and sugar until light and fluffy, about 3 minutes.

3. Add the eggs, one at a time, beating well after each addition. Beat in the melted chocolate. Reduce the speed to low and add the flour mixture alternately with the buttermilk in batches, beginning and ending with the flour mixture and beating just until blended. Stir in the vanilla.

4. Spoon half of the batter into a ziplock bag. Snip a ¹/₄-inch corner from the bag and fill the paper liners two-thirds full. Repeat with the remaining batter. Bake until golden and a toothpick inserted in the center comes out clean, 15 to 20 minutes. Remove the cupcakes from the baking pan, place on a wire rack, and allow to cool completely.

BANANA CUPCAKES
Makes 18 standard cupcakes

1²/₃ cups all-purpose flour
  1 teaspoon baking powder
¹/₂ teaspoon baking soda
¹/₄ teaspoon salt
  3 medium ripe bananas
¹/₃ cup buttermilk
  1 stick (8 tablespoons) unsalted butter, softened
1¹/₄ cups sugar
  2 large eggs
  1 teaspoon vanilla extract

1. Preheat the oven to 350°F. Line 18 muffin cups with paper liners.

2. Whisk together the flour, baking powder, baking soda, and salt in a medium bowl.

3. Mash the bananas with the buttermilk in a small bowl. In another medium bowl, with an electric mixer on medium speed, beat the butter and sugar until light and fluffy, about 3 minutes.

4. Add the eggs, one at a time, beating well after each addition. Reduce the speed to low and add the flour mixture alternately with the banana mixture in batches, beginning and ending with the flour mixture and beating just until blended. Stir in the vanilla.

5. Spoon half of the batter into a ziplock bag. Snip a ¹/₄-inch corner from the bag and fill the paper liners two-thirds full. Repeat with the remaining batter. Bake until golden and a toothpick inserted in the center comes out clean, 15 to 20 minutes. Remove the cupcakes from the baking pan, place on a wire rack, and allow to cool completely.

CARROT CUPCAKES
Makes 18 standard cupcakes

2 cups all-purpose flour
1 teaspoon baking soda
1 teaspoon ground cinnamon
$\frac{1}{2}$ teaspoon baking powder
$\frac{1}{2}$ teaspoon salt
$\frac{1}{4}$ teaspoon ground nutmeg
2 large eggs
1 cup sugar
$\frac{1}{3}$ cup lightly packed brown sugar
$\frac{1}{2}$ cup vegetable oil
$\frac{1}{4}$ cup milk
1 teaspoon vanilla extract
$1\frac{1}{2}$ cups grated carrots (about 4)
$\frac{1}{2}$ cup dark raisins
$\frac{1}{2}$ cup chopped walnuts

1. Preheat the oven to 350°F. Line 18 muffin cups with paper liners.

2. Whisk together the flour, baking soda, cinnamon, baking powder, salt, and nutmeg in a medium bowl.

3. In another medium bowl, with an electric mixer on medium speed, beat the eggs, sugar, brown sugar, oil, and milk until light and thick.

4. Reduce the speed to low and add the flour mixture, beating just until blended. Stir in the vanilla, carrots, raisins, and walnuts until well blended.

5. Spoon half of the batter into a ziplock bag. Snip a $\frac{1}{2}$-inch corner from the bag and fill the liners two-thirds full. Repeat with the remaining batter. Bake until golden and a toothpick inserted in the center comes out clean, 20 to 22 minutes. Remove the cupcakes from the baking pan, place on a wire rack, and allow to cool completely.

ALMOND CUPCAKES
Makes 18 standard cupcakes

2 cups all-purpose flour
2¹/₂ teaspoons baking powder
¹/₄ teaspoon salt
1 stick (8 tablespoons) unsalted butter, softened
3¹/₂ ounces (¹/₂ package) almond paste
1 cup sugar
3 large eggs
1 cup milk
1 teaspoon vanilla extract

1. Preheat the oven to 350°F. Line 18 muffin cups with paper liners.

2. Whisk together the flour, baking powder, and salt in a medium bowl.

3. In another medium bowl, with an electric mixer on medium speed, beat the butter, almond paste, and sugar until light and fluffy, about 3 minutes.

4. Add the eggs, one at a time, beating well after each addition. Reduce the speed to low and add the flour mixture alternately with the milk in batches, beginning and ending with the flour mixture and beating just until blended. Stir in the vanilla.

5. Spoon half of the batter into a ziplock bag. Snip a ¹/₄-inch corner from the bag and fill the liners two-thirds full. Repeat with the remaining batter. Bake until golden and a toothpick inserted in the center comes out clean, 15 to 20 minutes. Remove the cupcakes from the baking pan, place on a wire rack, and allow to cool completely.

LEMON POPPY-SEED CUPCAKES
Makes 24 standard cupcakes

2½ cups all-purpose flour

2 tablespoons poppy seeds

1 teaspoon baking powder

½ teaspoon baking soda

¼ teaspoon salt

4 ounces cream cheese, softened

1 stick (8 tablespoons) unsalted butter, softened

1½ cups sugar

3 large eggs

½ cup milk

1 tablespoon grated lemon peel

1. Preheat the oven to 350°F. Line 24 muffin cups with paper liners.

2. Whisk together the flour, poppy seeds, baking powder, baking soda, and salt in a medium bowl.

3. In another medium bowl, with an electric mixer on medium speed, beat the cream cheese, butter, and sugar until light and fluffy, about 3 minutes.

4. Add the eggs, one at a time, beating well after each addition. Reduce the speed to low and add the flour mixture alternately with the milk in batches, beginning and ending with the flour mixture and beating just until blended. Stir in the lemon peel.

5. Spoon half of the batter into a ziplock bag. Snip a ¼-inch corner from the bag and fill the liners two-thirds full. Repeat with the remaining batter. Bake until golden and a toothpick inserted in the center comes out clean, 15 to 20 minutes. Remove the cupcakes from the baking pan, place on a wire rack, and allow to cool completely.

VANILLA CUPCAKES
Makes 24 standard cupcakes

$2^1/_2$ cups all-purpose flour
2 teaspoons baking powder
$^1/_2$ teaspoon baking soda
$^1/_2$ teaspoon salt
$^1/_2$ cup milk
$^1/_2$ cup vegetable oil
1 teaspoon vanilla extract
1 stick (8 tablespoons) unsalted butter, softened
1 cup sugar
3 large eggs

1. Preheat the oven to 350°F. Line 24 muffin cups with paper liners.

2. Whisk together the flour, baking powder, baking soda, and salt in a medium bowl. Combine the milk, oil, and vanilla extract in a 2-cup measuring cup or a small bowl.

3. In another medium bowl, with an electric mixer on medium speed, beat the butter and sugar until light and fluffy, about 3 minutes.

4. Add the eggs, one at a time, beating well after each addition. Reduce the speed to low and add the flour mixture alternately with the milk mixture in batches, beginning and ending with the flour mixture and beating just until blended.

5. Spoon half of the batter into a ziplock bag. Snip a $^1/_4$-inch corner from the bag and fill the liners two-thirds full. Repeat with the remaining batter. Bake until golden and a toothpick inserted in the center comes out clean, 15 to 20 minutes. Remove the cupcakes from the baking pan, place on a wire rack, and allow to cool completely.

FROSTINGS

NEXT-TO-INSTANT GANACHE
Makes about 1½ cups

1 can (16 ounces) milk chocolate, chocolate, or dark
  chocolate frosting (do not use whipped)

> Spoon the frosting into a microwavable 2-cup measuring cup. Microwave on high, stirring frequently, until the frosting is the texture of lightly whipped cream, 30 to 60 seconds.

HOMEMADE GANACHE
Makes 2¼ cups

1½ cups heavy cream
 3 tablespoons light corn syrup
 1 bag (10 ounces) dark chocolate chunks (Nestlé
   Chocolatier Dark Chocolate Chunks 53% cacao)

1. Combine the cream and corn syrup in a medium saucepan. Bring the mixture just to a boil. Remove from the heat and stir in the chocolate chunks. Cover and let stand for 5 minutes.

2. Remove the lid and stir the mixture until smooth. Let cool briefly so the ganache thickens slightly before you dip the cupcakes. (The ganache can be cooled to room temperature, covered, and refrigerated for up to 4 days. Reheat in a microwavable bowl in the microwave, stirring frequently, for about 30 seconds.)

ALMOST-HOMEMADE VANILLA BUTTERCREAM
Makes 3$\frac{1}{2}$ cups

1 container (16 ounces) Marshmallow Fluff
3 sticks ($\frac{3}{4}$ pound) unsalted butter, softened and cut
   into 1-inch pieces
1 teaspoon vanilla extract
$\frac{1}{2}$ cup confectioners' sugar, plus additional sugar if
   necessary

Spoon the Marshmallow Fluff into a large bowl. Beat with an electric mixer on low. Gradually add the butter pieces, beating well after each addition, until smooth. Add the vanilla extract and the $\frac{1}{2}$ cup confectioners' sugar. Scrape the bowl well to incorporate. Add more confectioners' sugar, if necessary, to adjust the texture.

CREAM CHEESE FROSTING
Makes 3$\frac{1}{4}$ cups

Don't use this frosting for projects involving a lot of piping because it's too soft for that.

1 package (8 ounces) cream cheese, softened
1 stick (8 tablespoons) unsalted butter, softened
1 box (16 ounces) confectioners' sugar
2–3 tablespoons milk
1 teaspoon vanilla extract

1. Combine the cream cheese and the butter in a medium bowl. Beat with an electric mixer until light and fluffy, about 3 minutes.

2. Gradually add the confectioners' sugar and 2 tablespoons of the milk and beat until smooth. Add the vanilla extract, and the remaining 1 tablespoon milk if the mixture is too thick.

SEVEN-MINUTE FROSTING
Makes 4$\frac{1}{2}$ cups

2 large egg whites
1 cup sugar
2 tablespoons light corn syrup
2 tablespoons water
$\frac{1}{4}$ teaspoon cream of tartar
1 teaspoon vanilla extract

1. Bring 1 inch of water to a simmer in a medium saucepan. Combine the egg whites, sugar, corn syrup, water, and cream of tartar in a large bowl. Set the bowl over the simmering water, making sure the bottom of the bowl doesn't touch the water.

2. With an electric mixer on high speed, beat the mixture, still over the simmering water, until thick and fluffy, about 7 minutes. Beat in the vanilla extract. Serve this the day it is made as it becomes granular if it sits.

CHOCOLATE FROSTING
Makes 2$\frac{1}{2}$ cups

1 stick (8 tablespoons) unsalted butter, cut into 8 pieces
2 ounces semisweet chocolate, chopped
$\frac{1}{2}$ cup unsweetened cocoa powder
1 box (16 ounces) confectioners' sugar
$\frac{1}{3}$–$\frac{1}{2}$ cup milk

1. Combine the butter and the chocolate in a small saucepan. Melt over medium heat, stirring constantly. Add the cocoa powder and stir until smooth. Transfer the chocolate mixture to a large mixing bowl and beat with an electric mixer.

2. Add the confectioners' sugar alternately with the milk, adding more milk, if necessary, to thin, and beat until fluffy and smooth.

SOURCES

BAKING SUPPLY STORES

Beryl's
P.O. Box 1584
North Springfield, VA 22151
(703) 256-6951
(800) 488-2749
Fax (703) 750-3779
www.beryls.com
A wide variety of cupcake paper liners as well as many other cupcake-decorating supplies.

Candyland Crafts
201 West Main Street
Somerville, NJ 08876
(908) 685-0410
(877) 487-4289
Fax (908) 575-1640
www.candylandcrafts.com
A great selection of cupcake-decorating supplies.

Confectionery House
(518) 279-4250
(518) 279-3179
www.confectioneryhouse.com
A wide variety of the best-quality, solid-colored cupcake paper liners, melting chocolate wafers, sprinkles, food coloring, and luster dust.

Country Kitchen SweetArt
Retail Store
4621 Speedway Drive
Fort Wayne, IN 46825
(260) 482-4835
(800) 497-3927
Fax (260) 483-4091
www.countrykitchensa.com
A wide variety of colors of sanding and coarse sugars, candy decors, jimmies, luster dust, chocolate melting wafers, food coloring, and paper liners.

India Tree Gourmet Spices & Specialties
1421 Elliott Avenue West
Seattle, WA 98119
(206) 270-0293
(800) 369-4848
Fax (206) 282-0587
www.indiatree.com
Beautiful coarse and decorating sugars. India Tree products are also available in some grocery stores.

Kitchen Krafts
P.O. Box 442
Waukon, IA 52172
(800) 776-0575
www.kitchenkrafts.com
Wide variety of decorating supplies.

New York Cake Supplies
56 West 22nd Street
New York, NY 10010
(212) 675-2253
(800) 942-2539
Fax (212) 675-7099
www.nycake.com
Food coloring, chocolate melting wafers, luster dust, dragées, sugars, sprinkles, and some paper liners.

Sugarcraft
2715 Dixie Highway
Hamilton, OH 45015
(513) 896-7089
www.sugarcraft.com
A wide variety of baking and decorating supplies.

Wilton Industries
2240 West 75th Street
Woodbridge, IL 60517
(630) 963-1818
(800) 794-5866
Fax (630) 963-7196
www.wilton.com
A wide variety of baking supplies, including chocolate melting wafers, food coloring, paper liners, assorted sprinkles, sugars, and jimmies, and much more. Wilton products are also available in many craft, party, and some grocery stores.

PARTY SUPPLY AND CRAFT STORES

A.C. Moore
www.acmoore.com
Cake-decorating supplies and crafts. Store locations listed on the Web.

Michael's Craft Stores
(800) MICHAELS
www.michaels.com
A wide variety of craft supplies and cake-decorating supplies, including Wilton products.

Tower Hobbies, K&S Brass Supplies
(217) 398-3636
(800) 637-6050
www.towerhobbies.com
Craft supplies, including thin brass strips for making cookie cutters.

GOURMET CANDY STORES

Balboa Candy
301-A Marine Avenue
Balboa Island, CA 92662
(949) 723-6099
Fax (949) 723-6098
www.balboacandy.com
A great candy selection, specializing in retro candies and taffy.

Candy You Ate as a Kid
(866) WAX-LIPS (929-5477)
www.oldtimecandy.com
An interesting selection of nostalgic and novelty candies. Purchase large or small quantities.

Dylan's Candy Bar
(888) DYLANS-NY
(888) 359-2676
www.dylanscandybar.com
A wide variety of candies, including seasonal offerings.

Sunflower Food & Spice Company
13318 West 99th Street
Lenexa, KS 66215
(913) 599-6448
(800) 377-4693
Fax (913) 599-3787
www.sunflowerfoodcompany.com
A wide variety of colors of gorgeous chocolate-covered sunflower seeds.

Sweet Factory
2000 East Winston Road
Anaheim, CA 92806
(877) 817-9338
www.sweetfactory.com
A great selection of hard-to-find candies. Online and retail locations nationwide.

HOME DECORATING STORES

Pottery Barn
(888) 779-5176
Fax (702) 363-2541
www.potterybarn.com
Cake stands, both porcelain and wood.

Sur La Table
(800) 243-0852
Fax (206) 613-6137
www.surlatable.com
Bakeware and tiered cake stands.

Williams-Sonoma
(877) 812-6235
www.williams-sonoma.com
Cake stands and baking equipment.

PACKAGING AND BOXES

Dunwoody Booth Packaging
(800) 565-8855
Fax (800) 668-8010
www.dunwoodybooth.com
Boxes and packaging, including heart-shaped boxes.

Karen Tack is a cooking teacher and a food stylist for *Gourmet, Bon Appétit, Good Housekeeping, Family Circle, Woman's Day, Martha Stewart Living, Parents, Real Simple, Family Fun, Nick Jr. Magazine*, and many more.

Photographer **Alan Richardson** is the coauthor of *The Breath of a Wok*, which won two IACP Awards. He has photographed dozens of best-selling cookbooks, and his work appears in leading food and women's service magazines.

OUR WEBSITE
www.hellocupcakebook.com

Log on to our website to see our latest cupcake designs and newest candy info, to get updates on demonstrations, events, and book signings, and to fill us in on your own cupcaking adventures.

Goodbye, Cupcake!